Understanding
Your School-Age Child

By the Editors of Time-Life Books

Alexandria, Virginia

TIME
LIFE
BOOKS

Time-Life Books Inc.
is a wholly owned subsidiary of

Time Incorporated

FOUNDER: Henry R. Luce 1898-1967

Editor-in-Chief: Jason McManus
Chairman and Chief Executive Officer:
J. Richard Munro
President and Chief Operating Officer:
N. J. Nicholas, Jr.
Editorial Director: Ray Cave
Executive Vice President, Books: Kelso F. Sutton
Vice President, Books: Paul V. McLaughlin

Time-Life Books Inc.

EDITOR: George Constable
Executive Editor: Ellen Phillips
Director of Design: Louis Klein
Director of Editorial Resources: Phyllis K. Wise
Editorial Board: Russell B. Adams, Jr., Dale M.
Brown, Roberta Conlan, Thomas H. Flaherty, Lee
Hassig, Donia Ann Steele, Rosalind Stubenberg
Director of Photography and Research:
John Conrad Weiser
Assistant Director of Editorial Resources:
Elise Ritter Gibson

PRESIDENT: Christopher T. Linen
Chief Operating Officer: John M. Fahey, Jr.
Senior Vice Presidents: Robert M. DeSena, James L.
Mercer, Paul R. Stewart
Vice Presidents: Stephen L. Bair, Ralph J. Cuomo,
Neal Goff, Stephen L. Goldstein, Juanita T. James,
Hallett Johnson III, Carol Kaplan, Susan J.
Maruyama, Robert H. Smith, Joseph J. Ward
Director of Production Services:
Robert J. Passantino

Library of Congress Cataloging-in-Publication Data
Understanding your school-age child.
   (Successful parenting)
   Bibliography: p.
   Includes index.
   1. Parenting—United States. 2. Child develop-
ment—United States.
I. Time-Life Books.   II. Series.
HQ755.8.U53 1988   305.2'3   88-4925
ISBN 0-8094-5962-0
ISBN 0-8094-5963-9 (lib. bdg.)

Successful Parenting

SERIES DIRECTOR: Dale M. Brown
Series Administrator: Jane Edwin
Editorial Staff for *Understanding
Your School-Age Child:*
Associate Editor/Research: Rita Thievon Mullin
Designer: Cynthia T. Richardson
Picture Editor: Marion F. Briggs
Text Editors: Margery A. duMond, John Newton,
Moira J. Saucer
Researchers: Sydney Johnson, Mary McCarthy
Assistant Designer: Susan M. Gibas
Copy Coordinator: Marfé Ferguson Delano
Picture Coordinator: Betty Weatherley
Editorial Assistant: Jayne A. L. Dover

Special Contributors: Amy Aldrich, Dónal Kevin
Gordon, Michelle Murphy, Susan Perry, Charles C.
Smith (text); Charlotte Fullerton, Anne Muñoz-
Furlong (research); Nancy Lorince, Jayne E. Roh-
rich (copyediting); Louise Hedberg (index)

Editorial Operations
Copy Chief: Diane Ullius
Production: Celia Beattie
Library: Louise D. Forstall

Correspondents: Elisabeth Kraemer-Singh (Bonn);
Maria Vincenza Aloisi (Paris); Ann Natanson
(Rome)

Second printing 1991. Printed in U.S.A.

Published simultaneously in Canada.
School and library distribution by
Silver Burdett Company, Morristown, New Jersey
07960.

TIME-LIFE is a trademark of Time Warner Inc.
U.S.A.

Other Publications:

TIME-LIFE LIBRARY OF CURIOUS
   AND UNUSUAL FACTS
AMERICAN COUNTRY
VOYAGE THROUGH THE UNIVERSE
THE THIRD REICH
THE TIME-LIFE GARDENER'S GUIDE
MYSTERIES OF THE UNKNOWN
TIME FRAME
FIX IT YOURSELF
FITNESS, HEALTH & NUTRITION
HEALTHY HOME COOKING
UNDERSTANDING COMPUTERS
LIBRARY OF NATIONS
THE ENCHANTED WORLD
THE KODAK LIBRARY OF CREATIVE PHOTOGRAPHY
GREAT MEALS IN MINUTES
THE CIVIL WAR
PLANET EARTH
COLLECTOR'S LIBRARY OF THE CIVIL WAR
THE EPIC OF FLIGHT
THE GOOD COOK
WORLD WAR II
HOME REPAIR AND IMPROVEMENT
THE OLD WEST

*For information on and a full description of any
of the Time-Life Books series listed above, please
call 1-800-621-7026 or write:*
Reader Information
Time-Life Customer Service
P.O. Box C-32068
Richmond, Virginia 23261-2068

This volume is one of a series about raising children.

The Consultants

General Consultants

Dr. Kenneth A. Dodge, who provided expert advice on the chapters on social *(pages 60-83)* and moral development *(pages 84-115),* as well as on the developmental chart *(pages 136-139),* is professor of psychology at Vanderbilt University and a senior fellow of the Vanderbilt Institute for Public Policy Studies. He is also a member of the editorial boards of numerous psychology and child-development journals, among them *Psychological Review* and *Behavior Therapy.* Dr. Dodge has published extensively on the subject of social adjustments and peer relationships among children and is a specialist on aggressive behavior in children.

Dr. Paul H. Mussen consulted on the chapters on cognitive *(pages 6-21)* and academic development *(pages 22-51)* and on the developmental chart *(pages 136-139).* An authority on developmental psychology and personality development, he is a professor emeritus of psychology at the University of California, Berkeley, and director emeritus of the Institute of Human Development there. He is the co-author of the widely used textbook *Child Development and Personality* and has written many books and journal articles on the subject of child psychology. He is the editor of the *Handbook of Child Psychology* and has served as consulting editor to such journals as *Child Development* and *Journal of Genetic Psychology.*

Special Consultants

Peggy Brick, who contributed to the box on children's misconceptions about sex *(page 127)* and to the material on sexual development *(pages 124-128),* has written extensively on approaches to sex-education curricula for children and adolescents. As Director of the Center for Family Life Education for Planned Parenthood of Bergen County, New Jersey, she lectures to and consults with many civic groups on the subject of teen sexuality. She is a member of the Executive Board of the Sex Information and Education Council of the United States (SIECUS) and a consulting editor to the *Journal of Sex Education and Therapy.*

Dr. George J. Cohen, consultant for the material on children's physical development *(pages 116-139),* is a professor of Child Health and Development at George Washington University and a Fellow of the American Academy of Pediatrics. He is Senior Attending Pediatrician at the Children's Hospital National Medical Center in Washington, D.C., and the author of numerous articles on pediatric health issues. His volunteer work on child health concerns has been cited by a number of civic groups.

Dr. Sylvia G. Feinburg gave her expert view on the gender differences between boys and girls as expressed through their art *(page 73).* An associate professor in the Eliot-Pearson Department of Child Study at Tufts University, Dr. Feinburg has published a number of articles on developmental issues relating to children's art and is a co-author of the book *Helping Young Children Learn.*

Dr. Ronald Moglia, a noted authority on human sexuality, provided advice for the section on sexual development *(pages 124-128).* He is Professor and Director of the Human Sexuality Program in the Department of Health Education at New York University and a consultant to numerous schools and health organizations. Dr. Moglia's extensive writings about human sexuality include *On the Road to Good Family Life and Sexual Health,* the first kindergarten-to-third-grade curriculum guide based on children's developmental learning.

Dr. Bernard Spodek provided assistance for the essay on a day in a first-grade classroom *(pages 52-59).* Chairperson of the Department of Elementary and Early Childhood Education at the University of Illinois, he is the author of a range of books on teaching children, including *Foundations of Early Childhood Education* and *Teaching in the Early Years;* his articles have appeared in a variety of professional journals.

Dr. Robert J. Sternberg, IBM Professor of Psychology and Education at Yale University, gave his expert definition of intelligence *(pages 18-19).* The recipient of the 1987 Outstanding Book Award of the American Educational Research Association for his work *Beyond I.Q.: A Triarchic Theory of Human Intelligence,* Dr. Sternberg has garnered many professional awards for his research contributions to the study of human intelligence and has authored several books and numerous articles on the subject.

Contents

4

Becoming a Good Citizen 84

5

Your Youngster's Physical Self 116

Developing a Rich Resource

Most parents have mixed feelings when their child first marches off to school. That symbolic leave-taking marks the dividing line between early and middle childhood, the years between six and twelve. Gradually, the focus of your youngster's life shifts to his first academic tasks and his growing knowledge of the world outside your home. Suddenly, another adult—his teacher—has the authority to guide and direct him. And as he forms friendships, he may even—like the children opposite—seem to prefer their company to yours.

Still, family life remains very important to a child during these years, and your youngster will need your help as he rehearses and masters the intellectual, social, and physical skills he must have in life. When he does well, he will want to share his successes with you.

But along with his successes, a child's entry into school may underscore his weaknesses—perhaps he cannot solve math problems as quickly as he would like. At those times, he will need your active involvement and support in setting and meeting the kinds of goals that will enable him to get the most out of school during this important foundation-laying period of his education.

Children begin, in middle childhood, to see for the first time that not everyone shares the values held at home. Your child may ask seemingly endless questions about the family's beliefs. And, too, he may wish to test your opinions and limits when it comes to his own behavior; these are perfectly normal indications that your youngster wants the certainty of knowing that you still care enough about him to stick to a few guidelines.

This book tracks these middle years of childhood. Not only does it point out what is likely to happen as your child embarks on his journey to independence; it also explores his intellectual, social, moral, and physical growth. And it tells what you can do to help smooth your youngster's way.

The Mental Revolution of Middle Childhood

From the viewpoint of a proud parent, the intellectual blossoming that takes place in a child during middle childhood— those years from the ages of six to twelve—is as much cause for wonder as the unfolding of one physical skill after another occurring at the same time. Indeed, the mental development now proceeding apace in your child can be likened to his learning how to ride a bicycle. After a somewhat unsteady start, he is soon able to pedal off on his own—to use information to get results, to solve problems, to plan ahead. And if you are thrilled by his numerous accomplishments during this exciting period, no one could be more so than he.

Expanding horizons As he begins to discover how to use his mind, your young thinker expands his horizons. He grows ever more able to handle the abstract—mathematics, measurement, and time. Although as a preschooler he acquired a staggering amount of information about the world, he understood little of how his own mind worked or of the strategies that he could evolve for learning and for drawing on his growing body of knowledge. Now that he is older, he can juggle his perceptions of a problem at hand, a possible solution, and the steps needed to reach it. The first-grader who labored over every word in his first reader to break the code of written language will soon be the preadolescent who writes you a humorous birthday poem filled with wordplay and puns. So it is, too, that he will be able to figure out a strategy for stealing a base in a baseball game or

Shifting to a more adult role, a boy who no longer believes in Santa Claus keeps the spirit alive by filling his baby sister's stocking with goodies. As children learn to use logic and other intellectual tools, they begin to ask questions that show greater awareness of flaws in explanations of such questions as "How can Santa Claus eat all the cookies that people leave for him?"

to work out his next move in a card game after a surreptitious peek at the cards in his friend's hand.

As a further trend, older children come to rely less on magical thinking and immediate perception and more on their concrete knowledge of reality in their continued efforts to understand the world around them. Thus, fantastical explanations of flying reindeer, storks who bring new babies, and tooth fairies who leave coins under pillows soon fail to satisfy their questioning minds. Your child's outright acceptance of everything you said about Santa Claus or the tooth fairy only a few months ago may now be subject to considerable doubt on his part; something about these mythical figures suddenly strikes him as odd, illogical.

One mother tells how her six-year-old son asked her several times whether Santa really existed; she had never given a direct answer, preferring to have him draw his own conclusion. Suddenly the question took a definitive turn: "I do believe he exists," said the child. "But how is it that he can get all those packages to all those houses in one night?" The boy had applied his thinking to the problem of Santa's deliveries, based on his certain knowledge that events follow each other in a logical progression restricted by time considerations. Pondering the mystery, he came up with a solution: Santa stops time in order to get all his work done; and then when the job is finally finished, he starts time again and the world goes on. Thus, while beginning to apply logic to his magical thinking, the boy still had not abandoned such thinking altogether, believing that time can somehow be stopped and started at will.

The mind as sponge Why, you might wonder, do children make such major strides in their intellectual development in these middle years? As they grow taller and bigger, is the brain also enlarging, thus increasing their mental capacities? In fact, by five years of age a child's brain has already reached 90 percent of its adult weight; by five or six, much of a child's necessary brain and nervous-system development has already taken place. Then what accounts for such rapid progress? One contributing factor is that by this age, children have finally accumulated enough knowledge to permit them flexibility and a choice of strategies for effective thinking, remembering, and problem solving. As they gain more and more knowledge, children are also able to perform various mental functions with ever greater speed and ease—gathering information, storing useful material in their memory, retrieving information already stored there, and discovering ways to apply what they know to new situations.

A Growing Capacity for Laughter

A child's laughter is one of the happiest sounds a parent can hear, and the changes in a maturing child's sense of humor provide a fascinating guide to the growth and flourishing of his cognitive abilities and language skills.

As a preschooler he learned to identify correctly the people and things in the world around him and then took delight in playfully misidentifying them. Perhaps he referred to the next-door neighbors as Mr. and Mrs. Blue Car, or called your car a house. Whatever his little joke was, it doubtless elicited peals of laughter from him.

Now, in his middle-childhood years, your youngster's sense of humor will change with the maturing of his mind. Using his greater understanding of language and how it works, he will at first enjoy jokes that play on words' multiple meanings, including the knock-knock

genre and exchanges like "Call me a cab." "OK, you're a cab." Crazy riddles based on ambiguity will also appeal to him, as in this example: "How do you get down from an elephant? You don't; you get down from a duck."

Gradually, your youngster will develop the ability to perceive abstract levels of conceptual incongruity and to think logically about the misunderstandings and distortions of reality that lie at the heart of many jokes. He will see the absurdity of a customer telling a waiter, "Cut my pizza in six slices, I don't think I could eat eight slices."

In addition to jokes rooted in verbal ambiguity, elementary-school children love two types of riddles that have been classified as reality riddles and absurdity riddles. A reality riddle runs like this: "How many balls of string would it take to reach the moon? Just one if it's big enough." For your child to see the humor here, he must understand, at least in general terms, how far away the moon is so that he can picture the ridiculously large ball of string that would be required. To appreciate absurdity riddles, a youngster must be mentally nim-

ble enough to enjoy playing with absurd departures from reality, such as: "How can you tell if there's an elephant in the bathtub with you? You smell the peanuts on its breath."

Children in the middle-childhood years also demonstrate a liking for practical jokes and see fun in accidental mishaps. But the jokes that elementary-school children like most are the ones that deal with newly mastered concepts and require a little bit of mental effort to get. Second- and third-graders laugh at riddles that are deliberately ambiguous, because they are just starting to understand that words can have multiple meanings. Younger children do not understand these jokes, while older children, who have moved on to more sophisticated forms of humor, find them too basic. So, while your child may have reveled once in calling your dog a cat or recalling the time you slipped and nearly fell on the kitchen floor as the funniest thing he could remember, soon he will be having a great time stumping you with a silly question like: "Why should you wear a watch in the desert?" (Because a watch has springs in it.)

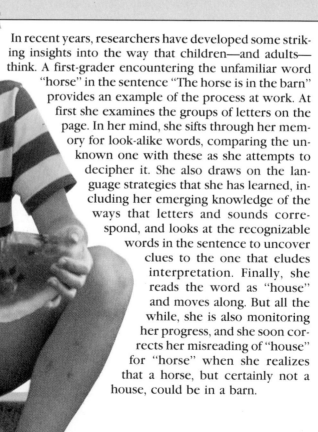

In recent years, researchers have developed some striking insights into the way that children—and adults—think. A first-grader encountering the unfamiliar word "horse" in the sentence "The horse is in the barn" provides an example of the process at work. At first she examines the groups of letters on the page. In her mind, she sifts through her memory for look-alike words, comparing the unknown one with these as she attempts to decipher it. She also draws on the language strategies that she has learned, including her emerging knowledge of the ways that letters and sounds correspond, and looks at the recognizable words in the sentence to uncover clues to the one that eludes interpretation. Finally, she reads the word as "house" and moves along. But all the while, she is also monitoring her progress, and she soon corrects her misreading of "house" for "horse" when she realizes that a horse, but certainly not a house, could be in a barn.

Perception and attention

Along with her growing ability to think, your elementary-school child becomes better able to screen out irrelevancies and to concentrate. These new abilities permit her to take information in more efficiently. When she was younger, you may have tried, say, to teach her how to form her name, using colored-plastic magnetic letters on the refrigerator door. She could recognize and accept her name, you found, when you used letters all red or blue; but the moment you deviated by substituting one or two green letters, she objected, no matter how irrelevant the colors should have been to recognition. Now that she is older, she realizes that it is not the colors but the letters that count, and she enjoys spelling out her name in rainbow hues. Similarly, she is able to concentrate, whereas when she was younger, her attention was divided. She could not watch television for long, for example, before getting up and roaming about the room or playing with her toys and then once more redirecting her eyes to the screen and away again.

As she develops the ability to focus her attention more efficiently, your child is also better able to evolve strategies for solving problems. When she was younger, she probably would have found it difficult to look at six similar drawings and pick out the two that were exactly alike. Preschoolers tend to glance haphazardly at the drawings and choose two impulsively, often in error. Today she will compare the drawings carefully, feature by feature, until she finds the matching pair.

Problem solving

Gearing up to solve logical problems of any sort requires that a child draw on perception, memory, and attention skills. Many experts liken the child's knowledge of routine activities—dressing or eating with fork, spoon, and knife—to following a script. The youngster creates the basic outline of what he is supposed to do and then pursues it automatically. Drawing on such scripts permits him to know what to expect in certain situations—and to raise questions when the unexpected happens. With new experiences, he develops new and more-complex scripts for a wider range of situations.

A magician who entertains at children's parties indicated that he much preferred performing for six-year-olds than for three-year-olds. The young children are all too accepting; if they find it funny that a rabbit comes out of a top hat, they do not question how the rabbit got there. For all they know or care, the rabbit might even live in the hat. But the six-year-olds feel challenged by the magic; they know that some trick is involved—that rabbits do not just pop from an empty hat—and they get very excited trying to figure it out. Still lacking the knowledge to solve the mystery, they are left with it gnawing at them.

Older children soon learn to develop strategies for dealing with problems, situations, ideas, or challenges with which they have had no previous experience. And they do it logically. For instance, a fourth-grader playing twenty questions will narrow down the possible answers. He understands that information can be arranged in a series of categories within categories. "Is it an animal?" he will ask. "Is it a land animal? Is it four-legged? Does it eat meat?" Not knowing how to use categories to reduce the possibilities, a kindergartner will ask haphazardly, "Is it a cat? Is it a bird? Is it a dog?"

Monitoring the process

One reason cognitive skills flourish in middle childhood is that children of this age have begun to develop what psychologists call metacognition—the ability to understand and regulate one's own thought processes. Your youngster has begun to evaluate her mental activity to determine whether she understands something; if she does not, she will doubtless ask questions. An experiment demonstrated the differences between first-graders and second- and third-graders in this respect. The groups were given deliberately ambiguous and incomplete instructions for playing a card game. Most of the first-graders launched into the game and soon were puzzled by the inadequacy of the directions; the rest of the first-graders never even questioned the reliability of the instructions after beginning to play. But the second- and third-graders thought twice about what they were being told to do, and recognizing the instructions' limitations, paused to let it be known that they lacked sufficient information to proceed with the game.

Getting it right

What seems clear about the intellectual growth of children in the middle years is that as their knowledge grows, it builds on knowledge they already possess, stimulating further cognitive growth and more efficient thinking. At times, the process can seem to proceed in leaps and bounds. All at once your little one will be able to set the table correctly, study for a spelling test, swim underwater, look a word up in the dictionary. And at the same time, she may be rapidly becoming adept at playing the piano, tennis, or chess—or even a combination of all three.

Challenged by you and her teachers to use her talents, develop her interests, and take intellectual risks, your school-age child will demonstrate again and again during these middle years that she is well on the way to becoming a thinking adult. •:•

Memory's Vital Role

At the same time that your school-age child is learning so much about the world and herself, her memory is becoming ever more efficient. In kindergarten, she may remember only four of the seven digits of her home phone number; but within a few short years, she learns the rules of countless games, knows the words to dozens of songs, and has memorized the phone numbers of several friends to boot. How does she do it?

Basic memory processes

Consider your school-age child's day. During it, she is a discoverer, constantly being exposed to all kinds of new stimuli. For her to be able to remember accurately a detail, a fact, a scene, or any other information later on, she must, of course, perceive it first. Then the information is compared in her working memory, or short-term memory, with relevant information from her stored memory; or if the new information is of no immediate relevance to her, it is included in her permanent memory for future reference, like a fact on file—or simply discarded. All this occurs within the span of about thirty seconds.

Some cognitive-development experts believe that your youngster's memory capacity increases as she grows older. Others maintain that it remains relatively constant and that children merely become more adept at recognizing, storing, and retrieving information. This then frees up more time within short-term memory for solving problems. Whether the credit belongs to an actual growth in memory capacity or to more efficient memory operation—or both—there is no question that your child's memory improves as middle childhood progresses.

The development of memory storage strategies

One important goad to your youngster's growing ability to remember information is her acquisition of strategies for storing it. These aids include rehearsal, or repetition, and the logical organization of information. Researchers have found that most first-grade children do not systematically repeat information to themselves to effectively commit it to memory. There will be some students, however, who have learned to use the device and who will spontaneously repeat, for example, a list of names they have been asked to remember. Not surprisingly, those already able to use the rehearsal technique will remember more than the other children. When taught it, most first-graders benefit greatly; but they will need to be reminded of it several times and challenged to use it before it becomes a real tool.

Memory retrieval

In addition to learning how to store information effectively, your school-age child will acquire memory retrieval strategies during middle childhood. These are, in a sense, mental prods that will help him recall or recognize information kept in long-term memory. This is not to say that children under the age of six lack memory retrieval techniques; they apparently form mental maps of physical locations, such as a playground, a shopping center, or their households. When asked to look for a missing book at home, even younger children can search for it, suggesting that they preserve a good mental map of the territory.

Older children will use a more sophisticated approach to retrieving a lost object. Your child, for instance, will search her memory as well as the physical location, combining several strategies in looking for her misplaced book. She might retrace her steps, restrict her search to a few logical places, or use memory fragments to reconstruct useful clues: "I was just about to pick the book up when the phone rang, so if I can remember where I was when I heard the phone, I'll know where to look for it." So aided, the child begins to construct, through associations, a web of interrelated memories. She gradually learns that drawing on or recalling a specific memory may help her remember other details.

Your child's memory, like every other aspect of her cognitive development, is strongly influenced by her evolving insights

Their many rehearsals have paid off for these proud young actors, as the Blue Fairy smoothly delivers her speech to the kneeling Jiminy Cricket while Pinocchio and Cleo the goldfish wait for their turn to speak. During middle childhood, increasing memory skills help your child learn numerous things—from the names of the streets of your neighborhood to the many verses of a favorite song.

Tricks for Improving Your Child's Memory

Memory is the key to learning, and you can encourage your child to develop his own memory through a few easily taught, basic techniques. Most, if not all, of the memorization strategies outlined here can serve as fresh, enjoyable learning games for your youngster. When they pay off by helping him with his schoolwork, he will doubtless be motivated to use them with greater and greater frequency.

Your child may develop some of these strategies on his own, or he may pick them up through observation, as he watches his siblings or friends using them. And he is likely to learn as well by your example. By employing memory-enhancing tactics in your own daily life and showing him how to apply them, you can actually improve your child's ability to learn.

One fundamental memory strategy, of course, is rehearsal, or repetition. Children can successfully use this technique to recall a variety of things, especially when they first enter elementary school. If, for example, your child has a list of names, ideas, or objects he needs to memorize, suggest that he try repeating them aloud a few times.

You can reinforce the process by participating in it. Repeat the list with your youngster and perhaps make a game of it by emphasizing the rhythm of the words, marching in place to the beat, or even making up a song based on the words. As anyone who has ever learned the alphabet song well knows, multisensory reinforcement like this effectively increases retention and makes memorization fun. Show your child how you use repetition. If, for instance, you have a telephone number to remember, repeat it aloud and then write the number down in his presence.

As your child grows older, he will probably use rehearsal spontaneously,

but occasional reminders from you will be helpful until the technique becomes ingrained. Studies have shown that once youngsters begin using the rehearsal technique, they perform far better on recall tests than children who have not yet adopted the technique.

Another way to strengthen your child's memory is to teach him how to organize information by category. Imagine that he has the following list of miscellaneous items to memorize: cello, armadillo, xylophone, lilac, walrus, bassoon, tulip, panda, violet. He could force-feed his memory by repeating these nine items by rote in the given order. Alternatively, providing he is intellectually mature enough to identify relationships, he could separate the items into categories—musical instruments, animals, and flowers—and easily commit to memory the short list of three items in each category. If your child has trouble breaking things down into categories, you can help by asking questions. For example, you might ask him to name the flowers among the nine items, then the animals, and finally the musical instruments. Young children rarely come up with the categorization strategy themselves. But once the technique is taught and understood, they quickly recognize its benefits.

The more complex technique of elaboration can make memorization still easier. It requires placing items, ideas, and facts into a larger context and then using a trigger to bring them to mind. For example, a child learning Spanish might be required to learn the word for duck, *pato,* pronounced pot-o. He could repeat the word over and over again, but he might remember it better by elaborating on it. Visualizing a pot will help with the pronunciation. Adding a duck to the picture will bring the sound and the meaning together. Thus the image of

a duck in a pot should be enough for him later to be able to recall or define *pato* correctly.

Mental imagery is only one trick to employ in elaboration. Help your child create his own phrases, sentences, and even little stories about the items he needs to remember. Give him prompts; if he has come up with a story, get him to draw a picture that illustrates it. The more vivid the story is, the more likely he is to remember.

Another common form of elaboration is analogy, remembering new information by paralleling it to something familiar. Teachers frequently use analogies to make points in class—for example, comparing insulation in the walls of a house to the layers of fat and fur that keep animals warm in winter helps the pupils remember the word's meaning. You can encourage your youngster to make up his own analogies, too, as a way of remembering.

Not unexpectedly, elaboration requires considerable mental sophistication on the part of a youngster. Although by the fifth grade children readily employ simpler memory techniques without benefit of any adult prompting, it is generally uncommon for them to use elaboration to stimulate their memories until they reach adolescence. Your child may not be ready to master the technique; do not force it on him by any means. The time will come when he can assimilate the technique and implement it to his advantage.

Whatever you do to teach tricks like these, you will be serving your young one well. The value of memory goes well beyond the ability to retain and repeat lists of facts, words, names, and the like. Through memorization, your child collects the data that he needs in order to interpret information and understand his world.

into how her mind works. She will find it easier now to look over a task and assess its difficulty than when she was younger; she will also tend to make more-realistic estimates of the time and effort necessary to complete the task. As well, her plan of attack will be appropriate to the task's demands.

Amassing experience

The growing knowledge base stored in your child's long-term memory plays a crucial role in the ease with which she acquires, remembers, and applies new knowledge. The more she knows about a given subject, the more points of reference she will have for each additional piece of information.

For instance, if your fourth-grader has already studied dolphins in school and has broken down her knowledge of the animals into several logical categories—what dolphins eat and where they live—she will very likely remember fresh details pertinent to material already stored in her long-term memory. And she will be able to add information effectively as well. Indeed, the youngster may even become something of a dolphin expert, an achievement in which not only she but you as well can take justifiable pride. ∵

As the school bus driver honks the horn outside, a girl searches desperately for her misplaced math book. Using a mature memory strategy, she has retraced her steps and remembered that she did her math homework the night before while sitting in the chair. A younger child might search the entire house for the book rather than proceed to the most likely location.

The Workings
of Intelligence

Perception, attention, memory, and problem solving—these cognitive processes will play an ever more important role in your child's intellectual growth in the elementary-school years. Although most youngsters make great leaps in their thinking processes during the middle years of childhood, each child matures according to his own unique timetable. Your first-grader may, for instance, become a whiz at adding and subtracting by the end of the school year, while an older brother or sister may have had to struggle through the second grade before acquiring the problem-solving skills that are needed for these mathematical tasks. Chances are that your children are not of equal intelligence, but each youngster will have his own strengths, as well as his own weaknesses.

What is intelligence? Psychologists disagree when it comes to the definition of intelligence. Alfred Binet and his colleague Theophile Simon, who devised the first intelligence test in 1905 in Paris, France, suggested that intelligence involved a "fundamental faculty." This they identified as "judgment, otherwise known as good sense, practical sense, initiative, the faculty of adapting oneself to circumstances." Under such a broad definition, in a fishing society, for example, the expertise of the captain who safely navigates his boat through hundreds of miles of stormy ocean qualifies as intelligence.

Some researchers believe that intelligence is a general ability that underlies a child's acquisition of knowledge, reasoning, and problem solving. Thus, while a youngster might have more information or experience with a particular subject than with another and hence score higher, say, on a vocabulary portion of an intelligence test than on the mathematics section, this general ability is still involved in answering both sections. Thus, in the view of some, it should be possible to rely on a single indicator of a child's general intelligence, such as the IQ, the so-called intelligence quotient, to predict her chances of succeeding in all subjects across the board.

In recent years, however, most psychologists have come to believe otherwise—that intelligence is not a single factor but rather is made up of separate and somewhat independent cognitive abilities. This, they say, explains why a child may excel in several areas—reading and vocabulary, for instance—but do poorly in another, such as math.

Some psychologists have also suggested that popular definitions of intelligence—and modes of testing children to determine their intellectual capacity—have overemphasized verbal and logical-mathematical abilities to the exclusion of others that are also important.

Howard Gardner, a psychologist at Harvard University, has identified what he considers no fewer than seven different intelligences. Gardner breaks these seven down as follows: logical-mathematical intelligence; musical intelligence; linguistic intelligence, or the ability to use and understand language; kinesthetic intelligence, as seen in the dexterity of a surgeon or artisan; spatial intelligence, the ability to think in three dimensions, like an architect or an industrial designer; interpersonal intelligence, as seen in a politician's skill at motivating masses of followers; and finally, intrapersonal intelligence, characterized by productive self-knowledge.

Psychologist Robert Sternberg of Yale University has also proposed a broadly based model of intelligence. Sternberg suggests that true intelligence consists of three sets of mental abilities involving analytical thinking, creative thinking, and practicality *(below)*.

Current tests and how they are given

While researchers attempt to design new intelligence tests that will identify a child's diverse abilities rather than focus on a few, the traditional IQ tests—especially the Stanford-Binet Intelligence Scale and the Wechsler Intelligence Scale for Children—remain in use by most schools. The tests feature similar questions that are designed to measure the rate at which chil-

An Expert's View

Looking at Intelligence Differently

How intelligent is my child? This is a question asked by most parents, and it is a worthwhile one. Since so many educational privileges—and ultimately society's rewards—are based on early evaluations of a child's intellectual abilities, many parents worry that less-than-hoped-for IQ scores or grades may indicate a mediocre future for their youngster.

But intelligence has many dimensions, not all measurable by current tests. Traditional IQ tests assess memory and analytical abilities, which our schools value highly. These tests have proved to be accurate predictors of a child's academic performance; but beyond the school doors, many other factors bear on life's achievements.

My own three-part, or triarchic, theory of intelligence proposes a broader definition of intelligence. Abilities fall into three major categories—componential, or memory and analytical; experiential, or creative; and contextual, or practical. Everyone possesses all three to varying degrees.

Componential abilities—memory and analysis—are very valuable in a classroom setting. Essentially, they are information-processing skills; children who use such skills efficiently and quickly are called "smart" by their peers and "quick" by their teachers. These children can promptly iden-

tify a problem, select an appropriate strategy for solving it, figure out the time and effort needed, and monitor their performance along the way.

Having strong analytical and memory abilities earns students a special place in our classrooms. Such students often score highly on standardized tests and do well on class assignments. These students are usually placed into top reading and math groups and occupy seats in gifted programs. They get encouragement necessary to perform well in the college preparatory classes in secondary schools, and go on to top colleges.

Experiential abilities—skills at synthesizing knowledge to create something new—are as valuable as the componential ones. They are responsible for a child's ability to use imagination, insight, and flexibility to solve problems; students who have strong creative minds will lead us into the future. Unfortunately, students rich in these skills may do less well than the more analytical students on tests, and teachers have few ways to reward creative effort.

For example, my daughter Sara's latest report card contained lots of satisfactory checks—adequate performance in the classroom. The teacher's comments reveal another Sara, a creative and expressive child whose interest in learning leads her to dren acquire essential knowledge, the amount that they already know, and their ability to learn. The youngster's score, her IQ, is still regarded as being a good predictor of her future academic performance.

Although the Stanford-Binet and the Wechsler tests are given on an individual basis, time constraints more often than not require that many school-age children take their intelligence tests in groups. Not suprisingly, scores from individually administered tests are considered more valid, since in a one-on-one situation the test-giver is able to establish a rapport with the child and can evaluate, among other things, her concentration, effort, and persistence, as well as the quality of her answers. The tester may also detect sickness, emotional upset, fatigue, or test anxiety *(page 36),* all of which can depress results. Under stressful conditions, some children may do better on an intelligence test if the adult administering the test is of the same ethnic background as they are.

How tests are scored   The procedure for scoring the IQ test is fairly straightforward. Once a child has taken the Stanford-Binet, for example, his raw score for each part of the test is compared with the scores achieved by a large sample of youths—a group of children of the same age who were selected to represent the U.S. population as a whole. A score of 100 represents the average score achieved by children in that age group. Although the Wechsler resembles

seek information for herself and to draw her own conclusions. At home, she always has a poem, drawing, or small project going—including putting together workbooks for younger children. Neither conventional intelligence tests nor report cards assess these creative abilities. If encouraged, children like Sara often find their métier, their niche, eventually as adults; but without some support at home or in school, they may feel that their abilities do not count.

Contextual, or practical, intelligence involves a person's ability to manage herself, her relationships with others, and her career. From my own experience as a teacher, I have seen students who performed well but not exceptionally in their studies, but who went on to have very fruitful careers. A child with practical intelligence is very good at meeting the demands of her environment; she can, for instance, study sample tests provided by the teacher and then figure out what material she needs to master in order to do well. She asks plenty of questions that relate directly to possible test items. This same child may apply similar strategies to other environments later on in her life. One of my graduate students whose academic work was acceptable but not distinguished found herself a great job soon after graduation; she knew well how best

to use her own strengths and to minimize her weaknesses.

Many successful adults whose intelligence is primarily practical will admit that they did not excel in school. In fact, success in some fields often has little to do with IQ or school grades. How is it, then, that a business manager with a poor academic record can be perceived by his peers as "brilliant" at what he does? IQ tests do not measure the practical intelligence required to succeed in many of life's endeavors—decision making, priority setting, and knowing how to get along with and manage others.

While current IQ tests provide a rough estimate of a child's academic performance, they are imperfect yardsticks when it comes to measuring intelligence itself, which covers an array of abilities—memory and analytic, creative, and practical—not entirely encompassed by any test.

Robert J. Sternberg, Ph.D.
IBM Professor of Psychology and Education
Yale University

Playing a duet with his teacher, this young cellist displays musical skill of a high order. Although standard intelligence tests cannot measure such artistic abilities, some psychologists maintain that these should be regarded as a form of intelligence, along with the verbal and mathematical abilities that traditional tests address.

the Stanford-Binet, it also provides, in addition to an overall score, verbal and performance IQs, the latter reflecting the test-taker's nonverbal problem-solving skills.

After about the age of six, your youngster's IQ score will probably remain fairly stable. A child who tests below 70 will most likely show a below-average result for the rest of his life, and the scores of one who tests above 140 will probably remain above average. However, the IQ scores of many children can—and do—show fluctuation between tests given during the middle-childhood years. Test scores may vary by as much as twenty points over a period of years. In certain instances, a youngster's IQ may fall or rise dramatically; a temporary decrease in the score may be related to illness, family upheaval, or other emotional stress.

Test scores, heredity, and environment

Although such intelligence tests are mainly intended to measure a child's potential success in school, the test scores have sparked an ongoing debate about whether intelligence itself is an innate, inherited quality or a product of environmental factors, such as intellectual stimulation, socioeconomic status, family stability, physical and mental health, and educational opportunity.

In some intelligence tests, black children have scored an average of fifteen points lower than their white peers. On the basis of this and other studies, several psychologists were quick to conclude that IQ is primarily hereditary and that whites are generally more intelligent than blacks. Other psychologists and cognitive-development experts have denounced that conclusion as racist; they attribute much of the score differences to the varying social and economic backgrounds of the children tested. These critics say, in addition, that test questions about items as offbeat as tubas, xylophones, and marimbas are unfair to culturally deprived children who have never seen, much less handled, such uncommon musical instruments. Within any ethnic group there is, not surprisingly, the full range of intelligence, from the lowest to the highest.

Some studies with white and black children of different socioeconomic backgrounds have indicated that factors such as family income and parents' educational level may influence a child's test scores more than race does. Testing a large group of black and interracial children adopted at an early age by well-to-do white parents with above-average intelligence, researchers found that these youngsters scored about twenty points above the average for black children in the particular region of the country where the tests were carried out. At the same time, studies with identical twins raised separately demonstrated that these genetically matched pairs have very close intelligence test scores, more alike than siblings or fraternal twins who were raised in the same household. It would thus appear that both heredity and environment have a hand in shaping a child's cognitive abilities.

Test scores—one aspect of the academic success story

When considering your youngster's intelligence test results, always remember that they merely reflect his performance of a particular task on a particular occasion. The IQ score has come to be associated, in too many parents' minds, with a fixed, mystical number that allows teachers and schools somehow to pick out the winners from the losers. As a way of de-emphasizing the tyranny of the IQ, the Stanford-Binet score has been renamed the Standard Age Score, or SAS.

Intelligence test scores give a good indication of how well a child will do in school. But, of course, intelligence is only a partial predictor of a child's success. Other factors include such hard-to-measure attributes as motivation, self-confidence, parental encouragement, and a child's attitude toward academic achievement. The youngster of lesser ability may, in fact, wind up in life exceeding in accomplishment the child who had been singled out as a genius by his test score. •∴•

2 Getting the Most Out of Elementary School

No doubt you want the best for your child during his elementary-school years. They can be among the most exciting of his life, a time when, like the fifth-graders exploring electricity with their teacher at right, his mind will be opened up to the wonderful world of ideas. But he will face new pressures too, in the form of increased competition, testing, and evaluation.

As a caring parent, you can do much to ease your child's passage, starting with the choice of the right school. In this section, you will learn more about what to expect from the classroom; see how teachers and peers play a role in influencing the quality of his educational experience; and discover how he may have his own unique learning style.

Throughout your youngster's elementary-school years, keep in mind that children thrive when they are allowed to develop at the pace nature intended for them. While there are many positive ways for you to enrich and broaden your young one's background, do not overprogram him. His chances to flower intellectually will improve if he is not harried and hurried. Happiness and self-fulfillment come from doing one's best and living up to one's potential. Your goal, after all, is not to raise the "smartest" child in America, but to raise a child who is happy and well-adjusted and motivated to do his best.

Making an Electroscale
Use your electroscale in
these two circuits. Measure the

Reading and Mathematics: The Cornerstones of Learning

Depending on your local school system, your child will spend one thousand or so hours each year for six years in an elementary-school classroom. Most of this time will be devoted to the three R's, or in today's educational parlance, language arts and mathematics. And with good reason. Basic competency in these studies provides the foundation for all future learning. For most children, learning how to read and write, add, subtract, multiply, and divide is one of life's first great challenges. Naturally, you want to do everything you can to ensure your child's academic success. You can best accomplish this by understanding how children learn and schools function.

Accepting individual differences

Children have gifts, aptitudes, and attitudes of varying degree; and largely because they do, they achieve scholastic progress at different rates of speed. Whereas one child may comprehend a new idea almost instantaneously, another may endure months of frustrating confusion before he grasps it. While one first-grader may seem to pick up reading unconsciously, another may learn slowly, painstakingly sounding out letters until one fine day he can read fluently. Similarly, one child may puzzle over addition for weeks before grasping the concept, while another comprehends on the very first day that it involves combining smaller sets of numbers into a single larger unit.

In all likelihood, the speed at which your child masters these skills will matter little once he has them tucked firmly under his belt. Remember, while the initial classroom goal may be to complete a prescribed curriculum, the long-term purpose of elementary school is to master the basics and create an enduring enthusiasm for learning. You can benefit your child by allowing him to progress at his own speed. Absorbing new knowledge and developing new skills can be thrilling, but it can also be stressful. You will be giving your child a great gift if you can tolerate his mistakes as well as delight in his triumphs.

The path to fluent reading

Fluent reading is nearly as involuntary an act as breathing. Yet at the outset it is never easy. A beginner must work hard at it

Making reading a pleasurable experience, an eleven-year-old boy enjoys a favorite book amid the rustling leaves of a sturdy tree. Although girls tend to score higher than boys in American elementary-school reading tests, the opposite is true in Great Britain. Offered the same encouragement, both sexes perform equally well.

until the process becomes automatic. Along the way, he draws not only on his growing ability to decipher words, but also on whatever background information he has that helps him understand the content. If, for example, your child is reading a book about a monkey at the zoo and he has visited a zoo and seen the monkeys, he will be better able to appreciate the story.

How reading is taught in school

Although some of the groundwork may have been laid in kindergarten, most schools begin formally teaching reading skills in the first grade. After decades of debate over techniques, many educators have concluded that a balance of phonics instruction (which teaches the association of sounds with letters) and whole-word recognition is the most sensible approach. The phonics method gives a novice a powerful tool for decoding new words. And the ability to recognize a few words by sight speeds the process and provides the child with immediate satisfaction.

Once a youngster realizes that there are consistent relationships between letters and words, he has broken the code, as it were, and henceforth his progress is likely to be rapid. By the end of first grade, most children can read simple stories with a vocabulary content of some two hundred different words. As phonics instruction draws to a close, usually in second or third grade, your child should have a solid grasp of the forty-four sounds—or phonemes—used in the English language. The upper elementary grades are then spent refining these skills and developing strategies for reading more advanced material. By the time your child is a sixth-grader, he may be quite an accomplished reader, able to enjoy novels, analyze poems, and understand the main ideas in social studies and science texts.

The value of reading groups

In most schools, reading instruction in the early grades takes place in small groups, where the teacher can give individual attention to each child. The teacher may introduce the subject of the selection to be read, giving the children background information that will pique their interest and help them understand the story better. She will then listen as each youngster reads aloud. Once each child has had a turn, she will lead a discussion aimed at enhancing comprehension still further. In most schools, students in the early grades are given workbooks that enable them to practice reading skills on their own and that keep them occupied while the teacher works with other groups.

Most reading groups are organized according to the students' abilities. The logic for doing so is to allow each child to learn with children sharing the same strengths and weaknesses. Still, because everyone knows which group is the fastest, as well as the slowest, this method can have the drawback of making the slower youngsters feel unnecessarily inferior. Teachers, and perhaps even parents, may have fewer expectations for these students, which can affect achievement in turn. Therefore, not all educators believe that placing children in reading groups is wise. If your child is in a reading group, you can make it a more effective experience for him by checking to see that his teacher evaluates her students carefully and reassesses skills often. In a good school, grouping is never rigid and students are moved ahead as they improve. Should you find that your child is not reading as well as you think he should be, speak to his teacher and look into ways to help him outside school, either with special tutoring or by giving him extra attention yourself.

Cultivating a love for reading

The nuts and bolts of reading instruction may be set in place in the classroom, but for most children the framework comes from home. Educators have scrutinized all aspects of reading skills and habits, including ways that parents can encourage their children to become ardent readers. Not surprisingly, their studies show that youngsters who read well and read for pleasure usually come from homes where reading is a valued activity. Having an assortment of books and magazines around the house, making frequent visits to the library, and setting aside quiet times for reading all encourage a young person's natural excitement about his emerging skill. As for television, often perceived as a competitor for a child's reading time, research shows that a moderate amount of viewing—up to ten hours each week—can actually improve reading achievement by introducing a child to interesting new subjects. History and nature programs, dramatizations of novels, even animations of cartoon strips can actually promote a youngster's interest in reading. You would be wise, if you are not already doing so, to guide your young reader's program selections.

There are several other ways to keep the fire of your child's initial enthusiasm burning brightly—or to ignite a reluctant reader's interest. Children's magazines are fun to read and can offer a youngster the opportunity to follow up on special interests and hobbies. Reading aloud to your child, even after she can read on her own, further sparks enthusiasm for independent reading, especially when you talk about the book together. And it allows you to introduce stories she would not discover by herself or might find too difficult to read on her own. Day by day you will have endless opportunities to point out to your be-

Books That Make Reading Fun

Reading for enjoyment is a cornerstone of literacy. You can help your child choose books that will delight and instruct her. To start, you might select titles from the following list by Reading Is Fundamental, Inc., a national nonprofit organization devoted to encouraging children to make reading an important part of their lives. The list was drawn from the organization's booklet *When We Were Young.* For further information on how you can encourage your youngster to read, write to Reading Is Fundamental, Inc., Publications Department, 600 Maryland Avenue, SW, Suite 500, Washington, D.C. 20024.

Grades One to Three

Allard, Harry, *Miss Nelson Is Missing!* Illustrated by James Marshall.

Cleary, Beverly, *Ramona the Pest.* Illustrated by Louis Darling.

Dahl, Roald, *Charlie and the Chocolate Factory.* Illustrated by Joseph Schindelman.

Hoban, Russell, *Bedtime for Frances.* Illustrated by Garth Williams.

Mosel, Arlene, *Tikki Tikki Tembo.* Illustrated by Blair Lent.

Parish, Peggy, *Amelia Bedelia.* Illustrated by Fritz Siebel.

Sendak, Maurice, *Where the Wild Things Are.*

Sharmat, Marjorie W., *Nate the Great.* Illustrated by Marc Simont.

Viorst, Judith, *Alexander and the Terrible, Horrible, No Good, Very Bad Day.* Illustrated by Ray Cruz.

Grades Four to Six

Blume, Judy, *Tales of a Fourth Grade Nothing.* Illustrated by Roy Doty.

Fitzgerald, John D., *The Great Brain.* Illustrated by Mercer Mayer.

Howe, Deborah, and James Howe, *Bunnicula: A Rabbit Tale of Mystery.* Illustrated by Alan Daniel.

Lewis, C. S., *The Lion, the Witch, and the Wardrobe.* Illustrated by Pauline Baynes.

O'Dell, Scott, *Island of the Blue Dolphins.*

Paterson, Katherine, *The Bridge to Terabithia.* Illustrated by Donna Diamond.

Rockwell, Thomas, *How to Eat Fried Worms.* Illustrated by Emily McCully.

Twain, Mark, *The Adventures of Tom Sawyer.*

Wilder, Laura I., *The Little House on the Prairie.* Illustrated by Garth Williams.

---

ginning reader the many ways that reading is intertwined with your life—billboards, highway signs, recipes, instructions on medicine, the newspaper. Get her to pick out some of the words she sees and have her decipher them with you.

Of course, in implementing any of these ideas it is important not to push your child or set an unnatural tone. She will resist pressure and notice disparities between your words and your actions. Just as the activities you choose spring naturally from your own interests, so should hers.

Helping problem readers

Despite publicity regarding illiteracy in the United States, the great majority of American elementary-school children do learn to read. And of the 10 to 20 percent who experience difficulty acquiring the skill, most will become fluent readers with time and practice. Some may suffer from a learning disability that interferes with the understanding of written language *(box, page 34),* a condition that usually can be overcome with individualized instruction. Emotional problems, ill health, or the use of a teaching method to which a child has problems responding can also affect performance. No youngster of normal intelligence need be left by the wayside. Should you have concerns about your child's progress, your first step should be to meet with her teacher. She can help you get a focus on the problem and may be able to recommend a course of action. Experience shows that reading problems do yield to extra attention.

The challenge of math

Just as a child enters elementary school having a certain familiarity with words, she begins first grade with some knowledge of numbers—she can probably count fairly well, for example.

Over the next six years she will learn a great deal more about numbers, mastering a series of skills that range from the simple to the relatively complex, not unlike her development from a hesitant reader to a fluent one. First, she must learn to understand one-to-one correspondences, to grasp the notion, for example, that the number 3 stands for three objects. Soon enough, she will build on such insights as she learns addition, subtraction, multiplication, and division. Later, she will explore fractions, decimals, and percentages. In the process, she will discover different ways of describing numbers: natural, whole, rational, prime. She will also gain some basic understanding of geometry, learning how to identify two- and three-dimensional objects, and to measure angles. It is important for you to realize that mastering math involves not only understanding the concepts, but also old-fashioned memorization. By the end of the sixth grade, arithmetic computations, like word recognition, should be automatic for your child.

Calculations and formulas, of course, have little value without application. School will show your child how to solve real-life problems, such as figuring out how many days a man would work if he worked five days a week for four weeks. Thus, even in first grade, your youngster is likely to be given simple word problems as a way of preparing her to address more complicated issues in later grades. The more complicated problems draw not just on skill in computation, they call for fairly sophisticated abstract reasoning as well.

These sisters, ages seven and nine, are building a medieval castle from a toy-construction kit and learning at the same time about three-dimensional shapes and spatial concepts. Such play aids them with their mathematics.

How math is taught Because of the way a young child's mind works, math instruction in grades one through three involves lots of hands-on experience. To un-

derstand place value, for instance, youngsters need to physically join ten small objects into one larger one. Your child will probably be given rods or other manipulative devices for this purpose and for work with other concepts. In the beginning, she may also be taught to count on her fingers. Such aids will help her internalize these transactions, providing some of the security she will eventually need to work in the abstract.

As part of their math education, children frequently participate in groups. The teacher assigns each group a certain cluster of tasks, which the members then set out to explore or accomplish on their own. Other work may be done by each child on her own, or sometimes with the teacher. The remainder of the time devoted to math (about 40 percent in elementary school) is given to the class as a whole. Educators believe this combination of activities is an effective one, since it provides children with formal instruction, the time they need for hands-on application, and small-group attention to concepts causing difficulties for some of the children.

The need for improvement In recent years, however, the math-teaching techniques employed in American schools have come under increased scrutiny because of the national concern that many children are failing to acquire the mathematical skills needed to cope in an increasingly technological age. To the chagrin of American educators and parents, studies consistently show students in this country lagging behind their counterparts in Asian countries, at both the elementary- and high-school levels. Experts have pinpointed a number of reasons for this, some involving the way mathematics is taught in the earliest years of school. One study, for example, found that grade-school students in China and Japan received much more instruction from their teachers than did American students. The Asian teachers spent more class time imparting information; in addition, a greater portion of the school day was devoted to mathematics instruction.

A number of solutions have been proposed to help American students sharpen their math skills. Among these are more homework, longer school hours, and an extended academic year. Some experts also recommend increasing the percentage of school time devoted to mathematics and having teachers put more emphasis on direct instruction. Most educators also see a need for a basic change in attitude among teachers and parents. Interestingly enough, the Japanese do not think their children have a special gift for math. Rather, they consider mathematical achievement to be simply a matter of hard work and effort, with

many mothers assisting their children with their homework or drilling them to ensure mastery. Americans, by contrast, typically attribute success in math to special aptitude.

Perhaps any fundamental change in the way math is taught and math skills are developed should begin at the elementary-school level, with teachers and parents modifying their own perspective and conveying to students the idea that, like reading, math can be mastered through diligence and patience.

Fourth-graders work together to solve a problem on their computer screen. Contrary to the expectations of some educators, the presence of computers in elementary-school classrooms seems to promote rather than hinder student cooperation.

Fostering math skills   Weaving math into daily life is one significant way you can help your child become comfortable with numbers and spatial concepts—and spark further interest. The opportunities for math-related thinking are abundant, although you may have to reflect for a few moments to get beyond the more obvious categories of money and time.

So that your child has opportunities to think mathematically, engage him in several appropriate household tasks. Cooking, for example, involves measuring in fractions, which you can show to your child as he fills, pours, and sifts. Similarly, taking the dimensions of objects around the house is a way to complement his understanding of inches and centimeters. As he gets older, you can give him real-life problems, such as calculating how many square yards of carpet are needed for the family-room floor. In fact, making up problems that involve actual needs and familiar situations may be one of the best ways to produce the kind of thinking that will help him in math. A younger child can count the number of commercials per TV program or the number of strawberries in each dish to be set on the table. When you

Do Computers Really Help Children Learn?

Although computers are increasingly common in early-childhood classrooms, experts are divided about their merit. While some contend that they teach logical thinking and encourage discovery-based learning, others claim that children do not need sophisticated equipment to master basic reading, writing, and arithmetic skills. And, these critics argue, because the software is geared toward routine drilling, computers often function merely as electronic tutors and differ from the old-fashioned workbooks they imitate only in the speed with which they provide feedback.

Still, in certain areas, advocates and critics alike agree that computers can have a positive effect. Studies have shown that when the programming allows children to initiate a sequence of events and then follow through on it, computers become excellent teaching tools. Because computers are fun to operate, children are drawn to them, and if given the opportunity, will come to school early or stay late to play with them. Also, computers seem to promote socialization. Teachers have noticed that children are more willing to talk about their work with one another when they are using computers than when engaged in traditional studies.

Finally, computers can strengthen youngsters' writing skills. On a word processor, for example, even a six-year-old can easily substitute words and phrases. When children show an eagerness to revise their work, their composition invariably improves.

shop for food, you can ask your older child to estimate the grocery bill or to record each price on a calculator and provide a total; in a clothing store you might enlist his help in figuring a discount on a sales item. And whenever you present a youngster with a problem to solve, work with him on strategy as much as on finding a correct answer. The strategy is what will stick with him, helping him to solve other problems.

Certain games and activities also foster math skills. Puzzles and card games give practice in finding patterns. A cube-type puzzle involves determining a pattern; more important, it demonstrates the need for persistence. And playthings such as model airplanes and construction kits train a child in spatial concepts.

Avoiding gender stereotypes

Although many math-related toys are often considered to be masculine playthings, it is important to offer them to girls, too. The practice of numbers, patterns, and spatial concepts is helpful in building what is sometimes called math literacy. The same holds true for computers—girls as well as boys need to be comfortable with today's technology. Encouraging math skills in a daughter should not stop with providing appropriate playthings. She needs to be told that she can excel in math and that careers in science and business are as appropriate for women as for men. Studies show that girls and boys score the same in mathematics throughout elementary school, but beginning in junior high school, the girls begin to fall behind. Although a few experts claim that differences in brain function cause girls to experience difficulty mastering abstract skills, the greater number of experts attribute the gap to cultural and sociological causes. A girl may be led to believe that working with computers is unfeminine, for example, or that being overly bright in math class in the upper grades will make her less appealing to boys.

Finally, examine your own attitudes, whether you have a daughter or not. If you view being good at mathematics as a gift, rather than as a carefully honed skill, avoid conveying this notion to your child. Math is no mystery, but it does require persistence and a tolerance for confusion. Cultivate both in yourself and your child and you will go a long way toward helping her, not only with math, but with all her schoolwork. ❖

Influences on Learning

Why do some children do better in school than others? Part of the answer to this commonly asked question lies with intelligence. But brainpower alone is by no means the sole determinant of learning ability—and it may not even be the most important one. Indeed, the attitude that a child brings to the classroom—specifically, his inner drive to achieve—is every bit as, if not more, important. Motivation can make a dramatic difference in the achievement of two students of equal intelligence. Even the brightest child in the class may not shine if he is not impelled from within to learn.

The spark of motivation

Where does motivation originate? Most experts attribute it, at least in part, to the values and attitudes that parents pass along and to the atmosphere in which the youngster grows up. Broadly speaking, parents who encourage their children to do well in school and offer plenty of praise for academic achievement tend to have sons and daughters who succeed scholastically. These youngsters set high standards for themselves and are willing to work hard to attain them. And, in the process, they discover a secret that will enrich them over their lifetimes—that performing to the best of your abilities brings satisfaction.

How to build that special spirit

At its most basic, instilling a positive inner drive in your child is simply a part of good parenting. Studies show that a warm, supportive home environment offers a child a strong incentive to achieve. In such a home, a youngster is open and uninhibited about her special interests and feels free to follow her curiosity. Although there have always been and will always be a few children who succeed in spite of their upbringing they are, alas, the great exceptions.

Too much discipline can make a child anxious and ruin her ability to zero in on a particular subject. As you might expect, praise for striving and for accomplishment is a far more effective motivator than criticism for apparent failures. This is especially true for a beginning student, who, after all, is weathering the sometimes intimidating climate of the classroom for the first time. Her confidence in her budding intellectual ability may be fragile, and she needs her parents to provide a buffer for the inevitable hurts and disappointments.

Promoting self-reliance from the very early years is another way you can prepare your child for school. When you allow her to choose the clothing she wants to wear, choose her own friends, and stay overnight at their homes now and then, you are helping her develop independence. She will come to see that she can be the master of her own destiny, and she will carry this understanding with her to academic endeavors.

Of course, there are other, more direct ways to kindle motivation. Do not be shy about making it plain to your child that you value her schooling highly, and listen attentively when she brings you news of her classes. It is also important to demonstrate the significance you place on intellectual effort and accomplishment. One way to do this is to fill your home with a variety of books and magazines, to read newspapers daily and watch the evening news on TV, and to make stimulating conversation a part of your daily life. Even a young child will enjoy participating in discussions about current events and important issues in the community and will want to offer her opinions. You can also talk about your own intellectual interests and, perhaps, your respect for those people who have attained success in demanding fields—teachers, scientists, physicians, politicians, and others. As in every other aspect of parenting, your actions will speak louder than your words.

Child psychologists have devoted much attention to what goes on inside a child's mind when she tackles academic tasks and how she interprets their outcomes. Like adults, children explain success and failure in different ways. Whereas one youngster may believe she succeeds through her own ability and effort, another may shrug off her triumph as due to a stroke of luck, or she may insist that the task was easy. Similarly, one child may blame her failure on her own lack of effort while another lays it to misfortune. Not surprisingly, the youngster who considers her victories and defeats as her own doing will apply more effort, set higher standards for herself, and achieve more than the child who constantly looks outside herself for a rationale.

Such attitudes toward success and failure are shaped early in

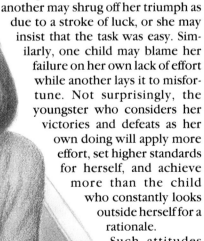

A first-grader proudly shows her mother a good paper from school. By displaying interest in her daughter's work, the mother is transmitting an important message: that she values academic achievement. Such strong parental signals are often all that is needed to motivate a child.

33

What to Do If You Suspect Your Child Has a Learning Disability

All children—and parents—experience some rough times during the early school years. But some youngsters seem to have more trouble than most: They are reluctant to practice writing or arithmetic at home; or they have difficulty remembering and describing what went on in school that day; or they just cannot seem to sit still and listen to a story being read aloud.

Years ago, such behavior was often dismissed as immaturity or even as a sign of limited intelligence. Now, however, experts realize it could actually reflect a learning disability, a disorder that interferes with the psychological processes involved in understanding or using certain kinds of information, especially as it relates to language or numbers.

One thing that is known for sure about learning disabilities is that they have almost nothing to do with intelligence—indeed, the most telling sign of a learning disability is a great difference between a student's overall intelligence and his performance in a particular area, such as math or reading. And they are fairly common: An estimated two to four percent of all school-age children have learning disabilities.

Parents who suspect their child may have a learning disability should call the school and arrange for testing and an evaluation, but they should also take the youngster to the family doctor for a complete physical examination to make sure the troubles at school are not caused by poor hearing or vision.

If the school's assessment indicates the presence of a learning disability, federal law requires that an Individualized Education Plan (IEP) be drawn up for the child. The IEP is essentially a blueprint for the type of instruction the youngster will receive, and—importantly—parents have the right to be involved closely with what goes into it.

If you have a learning-disabled child, prepare carefully for the IEP meeting with the school. Jot down notes about what you perceive to be your child's strengths and weaknesses, draw up a list of any questions or reservations about the course of action the school proposes, and perhaps set some goals that you would like your child to attain during the coming year. (At the same time, however, you should strive not to be defensive about your youngster's disorder or overly optimistic about any progress; parents do not cause learning disabilities, but they make them worse by causing the child to feel nervous or embarrassed about the condition.)

Although the evaluation and IEP are mandated by federal law, many states have also enacted their own laws addressing the needs of students with learning disabilities. Check with your state board of education to find out what additional services or programs may be available.

life and continue to develop throughout a child's school career. Babies, for example, soon learn that they are in charge of what happens to them when their parents respond appropriately to their coos and cries. And preschoolers who are given independence early on come to understand that they control much in their own lives. But even with strong beginnings, a child's outlook may be shaken by events in elementary school—peer competition, evaluations by teachers, examinations, personal frustrations. So keep track of your young student's attitudes; often children approach some subjects positively, yet approach others with the feeling that they are bound to fail.

Fortunately, you can modify the way your child interprets her role in academic achievement. Sometimes, simply suggesting that she try harder the next time—without making a big to-do over a less than desirable performance—makes a difference. In other instances, it may be helpful to provide new study strategies (page 45)—and to remind her that no one is expected to solve difficult problems immediately. Of course, you will want to be gentle in urging greater effort; she may, in fact, be trying much harder than you think. Often when children do not understand a new concept, they are too shy or embarrassed to ask the questions that might help them. Before attempting to change your child's attitude toward schoolwork, you should talk over her problems with her teacher. Your shared insights will invariably produce a remedy, perhaps even a redirection of the way the teacher handles your youngster in class.

The power of expectations

Running roughly parallel with a child's rationale for achievement are her personal expectations of success. Like the student who attributes her accomplishments to her own hard work, the youngster who believes she will succeed is in a good position to be successful. In contrast, a child who sets her sights lower, or anticipates failure, will invariably be less successful. Concern over doing poorly can also interfere with learning. Sometimes, a youngster has low expectations in one particular subject—math, perhaps. Naturally, she will try to avoid the subject that causes her so much discomfort, and as a result, her skills in that area suffer even more, with the problem feeding on itself.

If your child's self-expectations are low, there are ways that you can boost them. One approach is to show her new problem-solving strategies, such as how to break a task down into smaller segments that she can address individually. Another way is to reassure her of her own intellectual capabilities, perhaps by reminding her of her past successes. Point out that you are confident that she is perfectly capable of doing the level of work that she is currently struggling with. Here, too, a word of caution is necessary. Like everyone else, your child has limits, so you do not want to suggest to her that she is capable of doing absolutely anything she sets her mind to. No one is—and you will lose credibility in her eyes if you insist that she can. Instead, you might concentrate on helping her set realistic goals, praising her, for example, when she does break a task down into its component parts and tackles them one at a time.

The effect of learning styles

The manner in which your child takes in and responds to information also affects his schoolwork. Educational experts call this cognitive style, or learning style. Many studies have been done examining different learning styles in relation to academic performance. Highly focused thinking, called convergent thinking, is the mode that is generally most useful in solving elementary-school math problems. When tackling an academic task, a child who thinks convergently will proceed step by step, eliminating alternatives, and zeroing in on a single answer. Divergent thinking is more open-ended; a youngster who approaches problems in this manner may find many solutions, some valuable, others irrelevant. Because most elementary schools emphasize the ordered, logical, cognitive style typical of convergent thinking, nearly all children learn to approach problems this way at times. Those who seem to prefer it almost exclusively—and excel at it—are sometimes considered gifted. Divergent thinking is often associated with creativity, which depending on the child and the school may or may not enhance academic aptitude.

Another dimension of cognitive style addresses the question of how a child examines a problem. Does he see it as a whole or does he look only at its parts? When presented with a complex design, for example, one child may see only the large pattern, while another picks out the smaller shapes embedded within. Studies indicate that this latter type of thinking—known as field independent thinking—is tied closely with intellectual success; it permits the child to take apart a problem to arrive at a solution. Children naturally become more field independent in their thought processes as they mature, although some youngsters develop the ability more readily than others.

Impulsive and reflective styles
The aspect of cognitive style that has perhaps the most direct influence on a youngster's level of achievement is the degree of deliberation with which he approaches a problem. Some children—those who are said to be impulsive thinkers—barely glance at a problem before answering. Others are more reflective and weigh a question carefully before offering an answer.

To assess the two thinking modes, psychologists rely on a research tool known as the Matching Familiar Figures Test, or MFFT. The test-taker is shown a drawing of a familiar object and

How Anxiety Can Skew Results

Tests are at best imperfect measuring devices, and how they are given has a great deal to do with whether or not some children perform to their optimal level on them. The fact that your child tests poorly does not necessarily mean that he has failed to absorb the material.

When elementary-school youngsters encounter the world of testing and evaluation for the first time, many find the scrutiny intimidating and they worry about failing to measure up to standard. Often, these boys and girls develop an anxiety about taking tests that adversely affects their performance. As a result,

their academic skills and competencies are undervalued.

In one study, a group of fourth- and fifth-graders took mathematics examinations under four separate testing conditions. Each situation was designed to induce a different level of stress.

In the first situation, the pupils were informed that the test would measure their ability; in the second, they were told that the purpose of the test was to gain information about areas in which they needed more help; in the third, that they were not to worry if they missed some answers because no one was ex-

pected to get all of them correct.

Finally, as part of the fourth and least stressful situation, the children were told that the purpose of the test was to see how interesting the problems were and that they did not have to put their names on their papers.

Under the first two conditions, which are typical of many classrooms, the anxious children performed poorly on the tests, scoring well below the other students. But under the low-stress conditions, their performances soared, and collectively they actually outperformed their less-anxious classmates.

asked to choose an exact match of the picture from among a series of similar pictures. Children who answer within a few seconds make more errors than those who take their time. Experts find a definite relation between cognitive style and classroom performance. An "impulsive" youngster, for example, will often make more mistakes in reading than a youngster whose cognitive style is reflective. And in general, reflective children perform better in other academic tasks.

The question then is: What causes differences in cognitive style? Again, psychologists are uncertain; there seems to be no consistent link to any single aspect of the home environment. Some experts suggest that children with a reflective cognitive style are also those who are motivated to do well and are intellectually confident. It is, however, possible to teach an impulsive thinker to be more reflective. It may be helpful, as well, to identify more specific causes of impulsive thinking. Some educators believe that children answer questions precipitously because intellectual challenges make them anxious; these children are in a hurry to escape from tasks that make them uncomfortable. If your youngster is like this, your goal should be to find ways to alleviate his nervousness and worry over schoolwork.

Unique abilities   Being exceptionally bright naturally has an influence on a child's school performance. When coupled with the will to make it, her intellectual gifts give her a capacity to achieve far beyond the average for her age. Your child may be advanced in all academic areas or have a gift for one particular subject—solving complex math problems or writing stories and poems. She may also have special talents in nonacademic areas—music, art, sports.

But truly exceptional intellectual gifts occur only in one to five percent of all school-age children in the United States. Standardized tests and the observations of parents and teachers are the most common criteria for judging if a child's abilities are out of the ordinary. If your youngster has the capacity to concentrate on academic matters for long periods of time, or if she displays an aptitude beyond her years in any or all subjects, you should discuss her potential with her teacher. A highly intelligent child deserves an enriched course of study; otherwise, she may grow impatient with classes that do not stimulate her and thus may never fully develop her special flair. After considering her social development, emotional maturity, and personality, you might elect to have her skip a grade, take advanced classes in one area, or attend a special program designed for children with similar aptitude. •‡•

Why the Educational Environment Matters

Elementary school may be key to all subsequent academic achievement, but it is, at best, a human institution, shaped by the personalities and values of all who make it up, and subject to human foible. The dynamics of the classroom have many variables—the teacher, number of students, their intellectual level, and their socioeconomic mix. A sense of order and purpose pervades the well-run classroom. The walls are gaily decorated with the children's work. Books, posters, and other educational tools are everywhere. In such a classroom, an electric-like charge of energy and excitement fills the air, and the children are relaxed, happy, and respectful.

Your child's teacher One way to look at your child's classroom is to see it as a stage, with the teacher as director and the children as actors. When the teacher is good, the children give their best performances. Her influence is enormous. She arranges the classroom, organizes the lessons, and directs each day's learning. On the individual level, she keeps records of every child's progress and offers appropriate encouragement and praise—and when necessary, correction and discipline. Inevitably your child will develop a significant relationship with his teachers, and it is to them he will look during the day for academic standards and proper behavior.

How your child conducts herself at school is directly related to the type of person her teacher is. Researchers have found striking connections between teacher

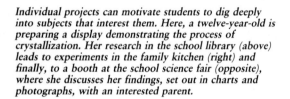

Individual projects can motivate students to dig deeply into subjects that interest them. Here, a twelve-year-old is preparing a display demonstrating the process of crystallization. Her research in the school library (above) leads to experiments in the family kitchen (right) and finally, to a booth at the school science fair (opposite), where she discusses her findings, set out in charts and photographs, with an interested parent.

and student behavior. The teacher who is prompt, respectful, and fair will inspire emulation.

Teachers are also models for learning. In one study, Regina Yando of Ohio State University and Jerome Kagan of Harvard University showed that when a teacher approaches academic problems reflectively, her students begin to think reflectively, too. Over the course of a school year, Yando and Kagan found, first-grade students of teachers who were thoughtful and logical in their problem solving became more thoughtful and logical themselves. The researchers attributed the changes, at least in part, to the positive effect of the children's becoming aware of their teachers' deliberative behavior, modeling their own behavior after it, and having the teachers then reinforce the students' positive responses. Some experts believe that it may be helpful for a youngster with an overly impulsive approach to problem solving to be taught by a more reflective teacher.

Educators also believe that a teacher can help a child learn by modeling intellectual strategies. For instance, a teacher explaining a social studies or history text might show students how she goes about summarizing and analyzing the contents. In effect, she would think out loud. Similarly, while teaching long division, she might

solve a problem on the blackboard, talking through each step so that each student can understand. And she will patiently repeat the steps, if necessary.

The influence of teacher expectations

The expectations a teacher has for her class as a whole, as well as for the many different individuals composing it, play a major part in determining academic achievement. Not surprisingly, a teacher who sets high standards and believes in her pupils' abilities will propel the youngsters on the learning path much faster than a teacher who settles for mediocrity. A good teacher shows her optimism in a number of ways: setting clear, challenging goals; teaching stimulating material; offering smiles, nods, eye-to-eye contact, and other positive feedback. Perhaps most important, she is judicious with her praise. The children want to please her. They respect her word because they know that she treats each child with the same uniform standards.

But teachers are only human, and sometimes their expectations may be clouded by such arbitrary factors as a child's gender, appearance, or even a memory of an older sibling who attended the same school. And a child's conduct in class can also affect both expectations and treatment; researchers have found that teachers prefer students who respond warmly to them and do not challenge or question their control. As a parent, you need to be aware of these prejudices. If your child is shy or unusually strong-willed, his teacher may not understand him as well as she should, in which case you should set up an appointment and discuss your feelings with her.

Open versus traditional classrooms

Classroom organization varies, depending on the preferences of the teacher and the policies of the school. Your youngster's classroom may be loosely structured, with no assigned seats and

During a peer tutoring session organized by their elementary school, a fourth-grade student (right) listens as a first-grader reads aloud during one of their regular sessions together. A child sometimes learns a skill more readily from another student than from the teacher, and the skills of the student-tutor often improve, too.

a great deal of student input into lessons. Or it may be more traditional—with assigned seats and the teacher in charge at all times. Educators differ about which system is preferable. Some find no difference between the two in terms of achievement; others claim that children learn more in the traditional format.

What does seem clear is that each style has something to offer. The well-defined structure of a traditional classroom may especially benefit children who are a little unsure or easily distracted. An open classroom promotes self-reliance and cooperation. And even in studies that show academic performance lagging slightly in open classrooms, the students generally report a more positive attitude toward school than do those in traditional classrooms. Choosing the style that is best for your child is a matter of weighing these variables against his personality. And the categories, of course, are far from absolute; chances are, your youngster's classroom will include elements from each.

In the end, the most important things are the ability and dedication of the teacher herself, whatever the teaching method and type of classroom. The most effective teachers are those who see to it that their students spend most of the class time on studies, who do not tolerate excessive interruption, and who make certain that the shift from one subject to another is swift and smooth. In other words, the best teacher is the one who provides the kind of atmosphere that makes learning possible.

Competition and cooperation

As you may have discovered already, peer influence extends into many areas of a school-age child's life and increases with age. Unquestionably, one aspect of this is competition in the classroom. As your child moves from the primary grades into the final years of elementary school, he will become increasingly aware of how his performance stacks up against that of his classmates, and he may also evaluate his ability in light of his peers' opinions.

A certain amount of competition can be a positive influence, provided that your youngster keeps his successes and failures in perspective and does not lose confidence. And there are ways to offset harmful competition by creating cooperative learning situations. Classrooms in which children investigate subjects together, in small groups, for example, seem to foster a cooperative spirit. The use of peer tutoring, when one child is encouraged to teach another, is another way that children learn the value of cooperative behavior. In such a situation both students are bound to benefit. Indeed, researchers have found that when older low-achieving students assisted younger students in reading, their own reading skills improved. ∴

How You Can Help

Your active participation in your child's school will increase her chances of being a good student. Parental interest sends a clear message—that education is important. But while your involvement is a positive force, interference with a teacher's work or a child's independence is not. Knowing when to step in and when to restrain yourself is a matter of experience and intuition. Being aware of a few general principles should make taking part in the learning process a constructive experience for all.

Involvement begins, of course, with the choice of a school for your child. Choosing one may be as simple as registering at your local public school. Besides being free, public education has several advantages. For one thing, the school will probably be located within walking distance of your home or be just a short bus ride away. Your child will make friends with classmates who live close by. And thanks to the school's proximity, you may find it more convenient to play an active role in school events. Of course there are other options. If you are unhappy with your local public school, you may be able to choose one in another district—although it is possible that you will have to pay tuition. Also

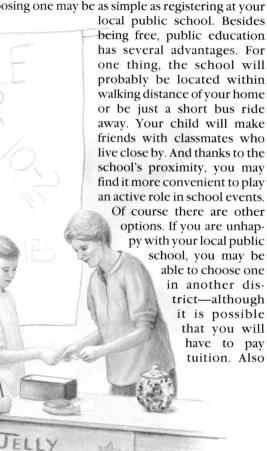

A mother operates a booth at a PTA-sponsored fair to raise funds for her child's school. Such parental involvement tells children that their mom and dad care about their education and instills in them the kind of pride that will enrich their endeavors.

Hallmarks of a Good School

A good school is what pupils and teachers make it—a happy place to learn. Good schools, of course, come in all sizes, shapes, and locations, but they have a number of features in common. The building is clean, well-maintained, and safe. While it may house elaborate resources such as computer centers and music rooms, what counts in the end are not the facilities so much as the opportunities the school gives the children to carry through on their academic tasks and to undertake responsibilities, including participation in the running of their school lives and representing the school in sports, music, or drama.

In addition, a good school has a dynamic leader who can command the staff's and students' respect and is accessible, fair, and engaged in their daily affairs.

In the classrooms there is an air of industry and enthusiasm. The teacher is clear in her instruction and offers appropriate feedback—plentiful praise for good performance and improvement, and criticism that is nonjudgmental. Most of the students' time during the school day is filled with active learning in academic subjects.

Other features of a good school may not be immediately evident. One is a serious attitude toward homework on the part of teacher and pupils alike. Studies show that homework does indeed help children learn, but only when the teacher is diligent about checking assignments.

Another characteristic of a good school is a respect for differences, so that the best in the children is allowed to emerge. To this end, girls and boys are assigned to learning groups on the basis of their performance, rather than according to IQ scores or teachers' impressions. And since nothing succeeds quite like success, the teacher expects each youngster to perform at his highest level.

keep in mind that many school districts now include so-called magnet schools for gifted or talented children, and that one of these might be right for your child. You can also consider private school. Among the advantages of a private education are generally smaller classes, which means that teachers can provide more individualized attention. Bear in mind, however, that a private school costs money that might better be saved for college and that it often has less specialized equipment than a public school. All the same, you may find that it suits your child's learning style exactly and be willing to make the financial sacrifice. You may favor a highly structured environment, and this, too, you can find in a private school.

Talk with parents of children attending the schools you have in mind; call the schools to request handbooks and curriculum guides. Then schedule a visit and speak with the principal.

Joining a parents' group Most public schools have PTAs—Parent-Teacher Associations. Joining such a group is a good way to get involved. These councils generally play an active role in school affairs, serving to make parents' concerns known and providing information to parents on key issues such as testing and special programs. In some areas of the country there are coalitions of parents, teachers, and administrators who deliberate major concerns affecting policies and curriculum.

The value of volunteering

Volunteering to help with activities is a wonderful way to learn more about how your child's school runs—as well as to show him that you care. Most schools rely on parents to assist in areas where they are understaffed—tutoring work or helping in the library, or chaperoning field trips. The school secretary or PTA president will know what sorts of opportunities exist in your youngster's school. If you cannot volunteer on a regular basis, look for other ways to contribute—giving a talk about your career during social studies, perhaps, or preparing a slide show or other materials for a special study.

Parent-teacher relations

Establishing a relationship with your child's teacher that goes beyond the casual contact you will likely have at school open houses is perhaps the most important single thing you can do to help your child do well academically. Some experts even go so far as to view a parent's role as a form of advocacy for the child's interests. Others prefer to think in terms of teamwork. After all, you and the teacher have the same goal—to help your child learn. You will want to meet formally with the teacher at least twice, once in the fall and once in the spring. Some teachers as a matter of course will schedule conferences with parents, while others wait until a problem crops up. Be prepared to take the initiative, if necessary. Good teach-

ers welcome the opportunity to get to know parents, because it gives them greater insight into their students, thus helping them do a better job and giving them welcome feedback.

Remember that your child's teacher may have to meet with twenty or so other parents. Before your conference, do some homework so that you can focus on the issues you consider important. By the first conference, you should be familiar with the subjects your child is taking and the books she uses, her schedule, and the types of assignments the teacher gives. Reviewing recent schoolwork will enable you to discuss your child's abilities more concretely. Make a list of topics you wish to discuss and jot down notes to jog your memory.

During the conference Perhaps the key idea you need to keep in mind for effective communication is that your child's teacher is a human being with strengths, weaknesses, pride, and sensitivity just like everyone else. Approach her with the same tact you would use during a discussion with any other adult whom you were just getting to know. Relax and listen attentively. Do not be overly defensive, but do not hesitate to speak up if you feel that she does not understand your child as well as she should.

A fall conference usually begins with a general discussion of your youngster. The teacher may want to know a bit about his home life, for example—his siblings, his hobbies, any special needs or problems he has. Be as open as you deem appropriate; such information can offer insights relevant to his classroom behavior, but there is no need for a teacher to know every one of your youngster's bad habits. The main focus of the conference should be the teacher's evaluation of your child's abilities in each subject and his conduct. The teacher should also explain policies regarding homework and inform

Learning to Study Effectively

Knowing how to study is fundamental to learning, and perhaps never is it more so than when your youngster moves into the fourth, fifth, and sixth grades. Then his homework is likely to include reading for in-class discussions and reviewing for tests. The habits he develops now are likely to be with him a lifetime. Here are several effective study strategies to share:

- Before reading, anticipate major themes. Think about the topic and ask yourself questions concerning it as a way of focusing your attention. Then go through the chapter introduction and summary, and look over any subheadings.
- Read slowly and carefully, and pause at the end of each section to elaborate on what has been read. Summarize what you have just learned and draw connections to previous knowledge and experience.
- Take notes while reading. Underlining and marking the books are fine if you own them, but writing down the major points helps both comprehension and memory.
- For tests, review notes; make up possible test questions based on key points. Reread the text when you are unable to elaborate on these topics.
- When answering math word problems, break them down into a series of steps and execute them one at a time.

Having a quiet, comfortable spot to work aids a youngster's concentration and helps him to take homework seriously. Provide good lighting and adequate workspace. References such as a dictionary, an almanac, and a globe are useful, too.

you of any major tests that will be given during the year. If she does not offer this information, ask. Toward the end of the session offer your own assessment of your child's abilities and discuss any disparities. And be clear about your expectations. For example, you might say, "I very much want his math skills to improve this year," or "I hope he will develop the self-confidence to ask questions when he does not understand." Finally, ask what you can do to foster the goals you jointly set.

The spring conference is the time to review your child's progress. Ask if his skills have advanced as they should; find out if the teacher recommends any specific summer programs. You will probably want to discuss plans for the coming year, as well, and make sure your child will be placed in a class commensurate with his abilities and reflecting his learning style.

At either conference, the teacher should be willing to show you your child's school file containing such information as test scores, teachers' evaluations, and reports from school specialists. By law, you (and no one else outside the school) have the right to see and obtain copies of this information.

When a problem arises

Occasionally, some children will gripe about school and make a fuss in the morning when it comes time to leave. In most cases, your compassion and tact will go a long way toward overcoming any resistance. If your child has trouble making the transition between home and school, he may benefit from having you spend extra time with him in the evenings, helping him ready his papers and clothes for the next day. His spirits may brighten, enabling him to go off to school happily. If he complains of difficulties in the classroom, listen sympathetically. Should the unhappiness last more than a few weeks, speak with his teacher. Often, the remedy is simple—perhaps a rule needs clarification, or his seat needs to be changed to keep him out of mischief.

If your youngster has a conflict with his teacher, the problem may be trickier. Sometimes just being able to vent his feelings to you will suffice; even a young child can learn that at times everyone must put up with less-than-ideal circumstances, and he may very well be at least partially at fault himself. If the problem continues, speak with the teacher, and providing your child is old enough and willing, have him take part in the conversation. His participation will make him feel that his opinion is valued. If a teacher conference fails to rectify the situation or if you believe a teacher is jeopardizing your child's achievement or lowering his self-esteem, you may have to speak to the principal about transferring him to another class. Whether you inform the teacher first is up to you. In any case, be tactful—the teacher's professional reputation is at stake. Although most administrators are reluctant to make reassignments, the principal is more likely to concur if you are firm and reasonable.

Helping with homework

Rare is the parent who is never asked to help with homework. What mother or father has not been called on to unravel a math problem, provide inspirations for a social studies report, or come up with ideas for a science project? But perhaps the best way to help your child in the long term is to allocate a quiet, cozy, well-lit place where she can do her homework *(box, page 45)*. And set aside a certain time each day for her to complete her assignments. Your youngster's requests for specific help can sometimes create a delicate balancing act for you. You do not want her to wallow in confusion; on the other hand, you do not want to do her work for her. The best approach is to listen to her questions and offer strategies and techniques rather than answers. Instead of telling your second-grader how to pronounce a word, help her sound it out. When your child has a difficult assignment, help her think it through; your intuition will tell you when to offer a definite answer. If she needs help frequently, consider hiring a tutor. Many parents find it difficult to remain objective while teaching their own children.

The question of rewards

Ideally, learning is its own reward. A child may read a book simply because he wants to know more about a subject. Psychologists call this intrinsic motivation, and every parent and teacher welcomes it. So motivated, a child needs no rewards other than your interest. In fact, studies show that holding out a gift for work that a child is already motivated to do may actually have the opposite effect, destroying his natural enthusiasm. Offered a reward for reading three chapters, he may stop there; left alone, he is more likely to finish the entire book.

Grades generally do not interfere with a child's motivation, because they are symbolic rather than concrete. At times, though, your youngster may want to choose a simple task over a difficult one that carries risk in order to get a better grade. The best tactic is for you to emphasize other aspects of schoolwork—the stimulation of learning, for instance, and the satisfaction of meeting challenges. Try to attend to your child's own reaction to a grade—whether it is pride or discomfort—rather than overpowering him with your own opinion. Often all you need do is recognize him for trying and offer appropriate encouragement to go on doing well or to improve. ∴

Homegrown Opportunities for Enrichment

Schooling need not stop when the school day or week ends. Indeed, the experiences of your child outside school can greatly enhance her classroom performance. Research suggests that visits to unfamiliar, intriguing places can increase her reading skills by generating interest in new subjects and broadening her knowledge. And activities at home—hobbies, private lessons, summer projects—can encourage her creative growth as well.

You will want to promote an open, freewheeling approach to out-of-school learning. Do not think of creativity, however, as being strictly limited to artistic endeavors. Rather, regard it as a fresh way of getting to know the world. When a child thinks creatively, she generates ideas and sees relationships among disparate concepts; indeed, she dares to be bold. Unconcerned about right and wrong answers, she finds the unknown challenging and fun rather than scary. You can promote this quality in your child by being inquisitive and flexible yourself.

Family outings

One way of fueling your child's interests is to take her to historical sites, museums, and science exhibitions, and to concerts, plays, and other performances. But do so as the child's spirit moves you. You will not want to nip in the bud a growing enthusiasm for such outings by insisting on her compliance all the time, especially if she has in mind a day of play with her best friend. When she accompanies you willingly, she will be in a mood to make discoveries and to appreciate art and beauty.

Your child can expand her horizons on a visit to almost any new place. You might consider taking an amble through a neighborhood neither of you knows, for example, or shopping at an outdoor market, or touring a local factory. So that your youngster will get the most out of such experiences, always talk about them beforehand and afterward, and ask the kind of questions that surprise and produce reflection.

Using television as an educational tool

Television is a fact of life in today's society and despite its obvious pitfalls, it can be used to stimulate your child's intellectual growth; for starters, all that is required is some monitored viewing. After all, many shows explore places and ways of life that she might not otherwise encounter, and good drama always generates powerful emotions. Instead of allowing her to flip through the channels or sit for hours watching cartoons or age-inappropriate shows, take a few minutes to study the weekly programming guide, perhaps with her at your side, and plan a schedule of good viewing. If you have time, watch the shows with her, so that the two of you can talk them over afterward.

As part of a demonstration at a colonial farm fair, a brother and sister and their father learn firsthand how early-American settlers dipped candles. Outings to historic sites not only help children understand the past better but also stimulate them to think critically about the present.

Ask questions that give her food for thought: "Did you know the story would end that way?" or "What did you think of the costumes?" Encourage moral and ethical evaluations, too. Ask her if she liked the way the hero worked out her conflict and what she would have done under similar circumstances.

The role of hobbies and games

Childhood hobbies can become lifelong passions, and sometimes even lead to a particular career or field of study. During these middle-childhood years, a youngster often turns into an avid collector. In the process, she learns not only about the items in her collections, but also—perhaps with a little input from you—about how to classify objects, a cognitive skill important in school. If your child has been bitten by the collecting bug, indulge her as much as space and budget permit. You might provide shelves or scrapbooks to store her collections; or you might show her how seashells, for example, can be grouped by size, color, shape, or geographic origin. Collections can lead a child to books, too; as her interest grows, a butterfly enthusiast is likely to want to read more about the insect.

Games also can play a role in a youngster's intellectual development. Card games, like collections, often involve classifying skills; in rummy, for instance, children learn to group the deck by suit or rank. Word games build vocabulary and spelling skills, and many board games give practice in counting, developing winning strategies, and making decisions.

Private lessons

As part of your child's enrichment, you may wish to have her take lessons of one sort or another. Many parents find that the discipline of regular practice carries over into other aspects of their youngsters' lives. If you gear your expectations to your child's abilities and appreciate that this age should be a time for exploration, lessons can offer her opportunities to express herself in new ways.

Chances are that if you like music or play an instrument yourself, your child will want to follow suit. At first, she may enjoy experimenting with simple instruments—perhaps a pipe or an autoharp. By about the age of eight, she may be ready for the piano, a flute, a violin, or other instrument. Although you can get professional advice about which instruments suit her best, let her make the choice. In doing so, you are allowing her own interest and enthusiasm to spark the learning process. Once lessons start, practice sessions should be fairly short. Have her begin with about ten minutes a day for the first few months, then increase the session in small increments until she is playing for thirty to forty-five minutes each day.

Your child might also enjoy art lessons, even if she has no particular urge to be a painter or sculptor. Interestingly enough, experts believe that artistic endeavors foster creativity of other sorts. Painting, drawing, and modeling with clay, it seems, give a young person the chance to develop her own way of organizing information and elaborating on themes. You might look for an art class that allows your youngster to work intensely in one specific material. Research suggests that in-depth exploration helps nurture creative impulses better than involvement with several media at once.

Summertime

When school shuts down for summer vacation, a whole new learning opportunity comes your child's way. For children, summer can be a very special time—a chance to indulge interests, to explore new vistas, or simply to be independent, dream dreams, and revel in the delicious pleasure of being free of school restraints.

How you and your youngster arrange these months depends, of course, on many factors—his tastes and temperament, whether or not both parents work, and what activities and facilities are available in the community. Each summer need not be the same. He may enjoy day camp one year, a month with his grandparents the next, and a summer of unstructured fun the third.

Children want and need to be competent, and summer is the perfect time to acquire new ego-boosting skills, such as carpentry, baking, or bicycle repair. Your school may offer enrichment classes in various nonacademic subjects. Day-camp programs may provide a potpourri of enterprises or focus on a single area, such as baseball or music. Overnight camps may combine camping programs with emphasis on woodcraft and outdoor skills, or they may be very specific, concentrating on remedial work or special programs in the arts. Keep in mind, though, that some youngsters may benefit more from a complete break in their highly structured lives. A summer in which each day is unencumbered with responsibility might turn out to be one of the greatest gifts you can bestow on your school-age child. ❖

Standing in front of weather station display modules in a science museum, children observe satellite photographs of cloud formations high above the earth. Such hands-on demonstrations enrich lessons learned in the classroom.

A Dynamic Day in First Grade

First-grade year is a journey to discovery. For most six-year-olds, the academic progress they make will be unequaled in any other year for the rest of their lives. In the opening days of school, many youngsters have to be told over and over again how to put their name at the top of a sheet of paper. Yet by springtime, these very same children are writing short narratives, covering the pages of their notebooks with neatly spaced, properly spelled words. And what is more, they are reading simple books and are comfortable with the basic processes of mathematics and science.

Much of the incentive for this amazing growth comes from the children themselves. Most six-year-olds are eager to learn and sometimes seem to drink in new skills and information. Still, their remarkable progress does not happen in a vacuum. Rather, it takes

Introducing New Words

In the opening session of a morning devoted to language arts, several children eagerly respond to a question the teacher has asked about the common elements of the new vocabulary words on the blackboard. All the words share the common vowel sound symbolized by the letters ie.

place within a carefully planned structure that encompasses a variety of approaches to learning: quiet and active work, group and individual study, teacher-directed and independent efforts. And at the same time, the children are absorbing social skills, including lessons in responsibility and self-discipline.

In all of this, of course, the teacher plays a crucial part. She is many things to each child—educator, parent, police officer, referee, doctor, and nurse. A good first-grade teacher is able to be warm and caring as well as challenging and serious. At least one study suggests the far-reaching impact of such an individual. In a survey of adults who had attended the same elementary school, a large majority of those who had studied with an unusually committed first-grade teacher reported pursuing their lifetime schooling further than those who had been in other classes. A positive first-grade experience lays a strong educational foundation by establishing a solid base of skills and nurturing a child's natural enthusiasm for learning.

The following pages take you through a day in the life of a typical first-grade class. During the six-hour-long school day, the youngsters concentrate on the building blocks of academic knowledge—language arts, mathematics, and science. But for balance and enrichment, they also delve into music, art, social studies, and physical education, and visit the computer lab and library. The classroom is a beehive of activity, informal but always organized. Often an audible hum of energy and excitement fills the air. This is indeed an environment that fosters thinking and self-confidence and at its best, a lifelong love of learning.

Developing reading skills

During the reading portion of language arts, the class divides into
small groups. Above, one group takes turns reading aloud with the
teacher; other groups (not shown) are reading elsewhere in the
room with aides. Afterward, the students return to their seats and
answer questions about the story, referring to their books as needed
(left). Finally, they reinforce their comprehension by drawing
pictures of story words (below) listed on the blackboard.

Developing oral skills

Language arts includes dramatic activities such as the puppet show these girls are performing. The students first make up a story, then act it out with puppets. The exercise develops speaking skills and storytelling; it also helps children learn to listen.

Reviewing new words in a fresh way

The class reviews vocabulary words from their readers. The exercise is designed to help the children master new vocabulary— the teacher repeats each word several times and uses it in a sentence to make sure that the meaning is well understood. Although this is not a test, the boy in front has put up a wall of books to keep the girl next to him from copying his responses.

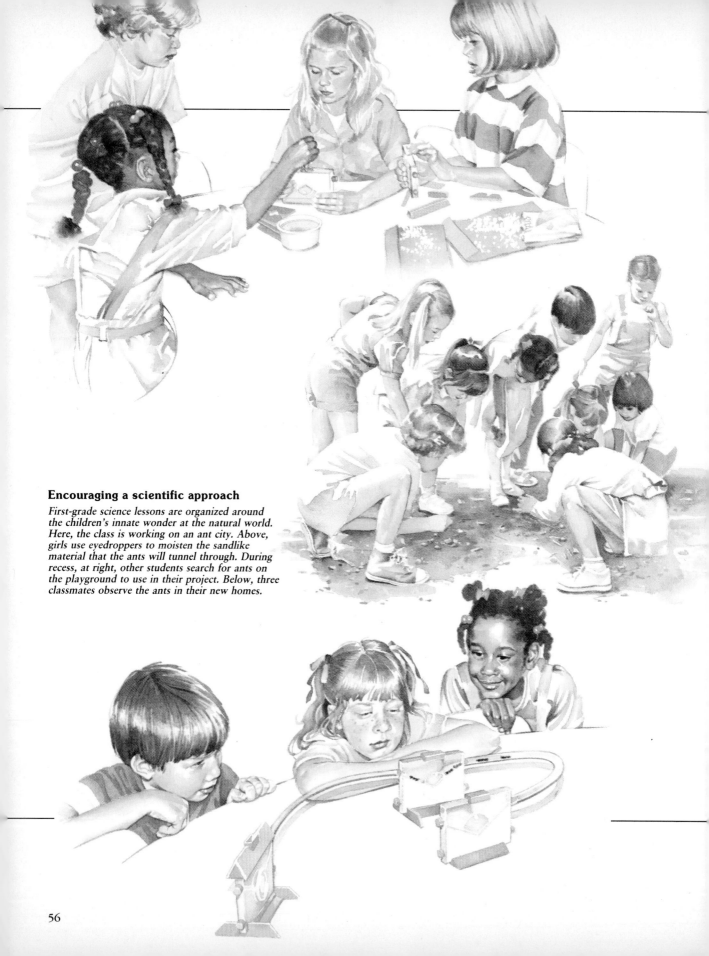

Encouraging a scientific approach

First-grade science lessons are organized around the children's innate wonder at the natural world. Here, the class is working on an ant city. Above, girls use eyedroppers to moisten the sandlike material that the ants will tunnel through. During recess, at right, other students search for ants on the playground to use in their project. Below, three classmates observe the ants in their new homes.

56

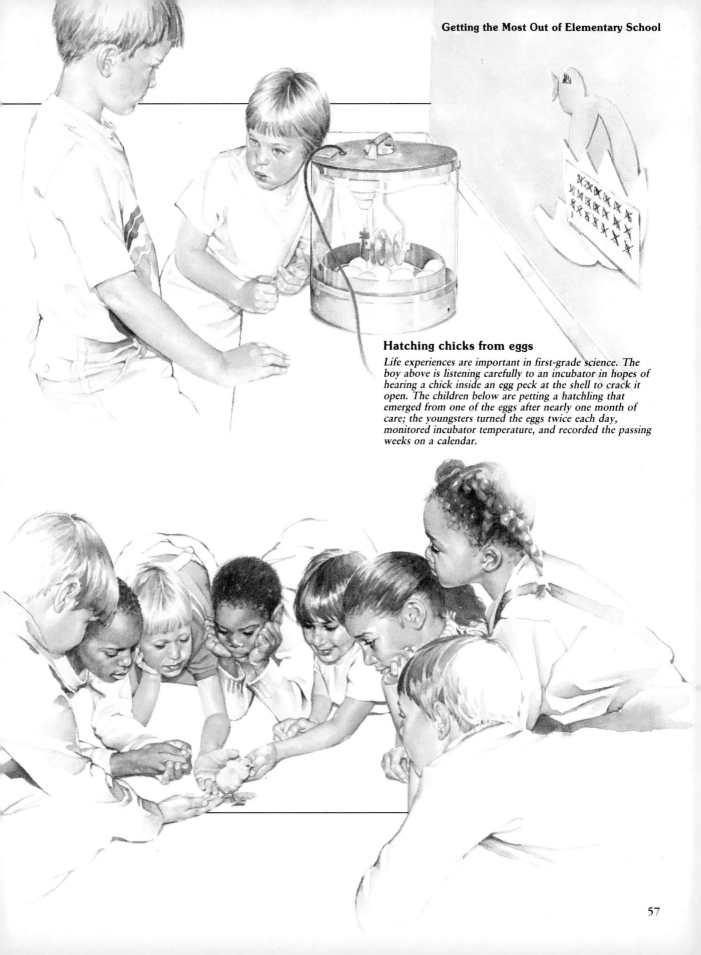

Hatching chicks from eggs

Life experiences are important in first-grade science. The boy above is listening carefully to an incubator in hopes of hearing a chick inside an egg peck at the shell to crack it open. The children below are petting a hatchling that emerged from one of the eggs after nearly one month of care; the youngsters turned the eggs twice each day, monitored incubator temperature, and recorded the passing weeks on a calendar.

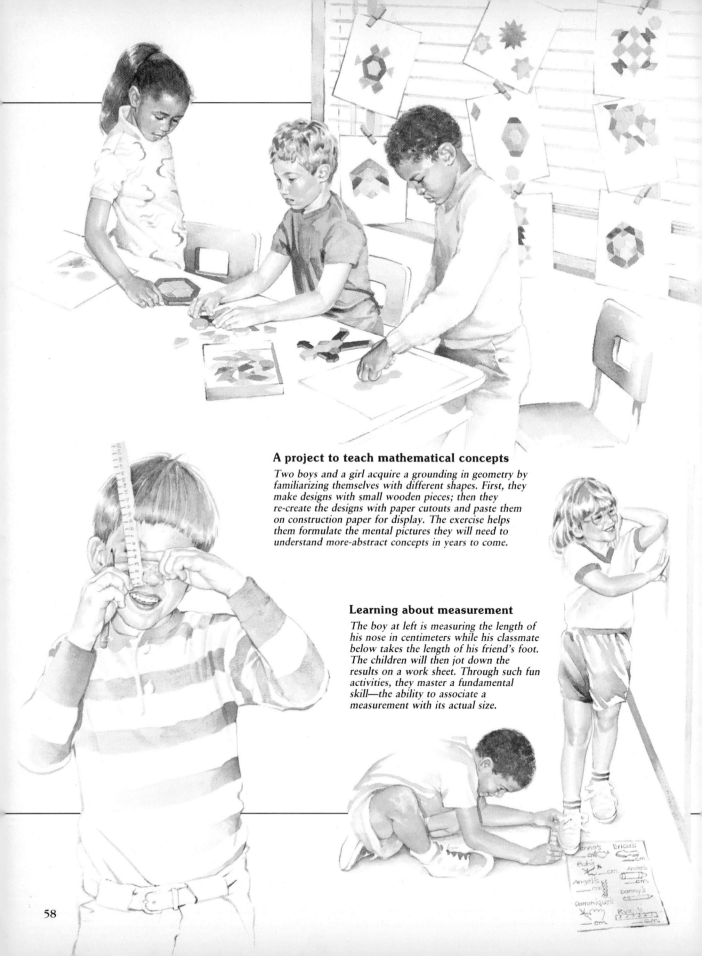

A project to teach mathematical concepts

Two boys and a girl acquire a grounding in geometry by familiarizing themselves with different shapes. First, they make designs with small wooden pieces; then they re-create the designs with paper cutouts and paste them on construction paper for display. The exercise helps them formulate the mental pictures they will need to understand more-abstract concepts in years to come.

Learning about measurement

The boy at left is measuring the length of his nose in centimeters while his classmate below takes the length of his friend's foot. The children will then jot down the results on a work sheet. Through such fun activities, they master a fundamental skill—the ability to associate a measurement with its actual size.

Using manipulative devices to understand numbers

These children are learning about numbers; the girl is computing an answer for her work sheet by counting on her fingers; the boys are counting with plastic rods. The long rods represent units of ten, the short ones stand for single units. Some parents are concerned when their children count on their fingers, but the technique is just as useful as any other manipulative device and is perfectly acceptable.

A warm ending to a fruitful day

The busy school day over, the students line up to go home. In their backpacks, they are carrying work they have completed to show to their parents. As the children go out the door, the teacher gives two hard workers an appreciative hug. Tomorrow, another busy day of learning will begin for the first-graders.

3 Out of the Nest and into the World

If not yet an independent person, your school-age child is now better able to cope on his own. As his horizon stretches beyond the narrow confines of home and family to the larger community of school and neighborhood, his peers will play an increasingly significant role in his life, influencing not only the clothing that he wears and his haircut, but his attitudes and his values as well. It is small wonder. By the age of eleven or twelve, most children are spending half their waking hours in the company of friends.

At the same time, the nature of your relationship with him will also change, perhaps most visibly in terms of the decrease in the amount of time you now need to spend supervising or entertaining him. Instead, like the father at right, you will find yourself doing more advising and counseling. Children adopt the standards and behavior of the people they love or admire in their daily lives, and as your youngster matures, you and others will become ever more important to him as models.

These middle childhood relationships fulfill the critical developmental function of teaching your youngster how to become a member of society. While playing with peers, a child is free from parental authority and is forced to learn how to make and keep friends, negotiate, come to decisions of his own, resolve conflicts, and compromise. And by imitating appropriate adult behavior, boys and girls refine their understanding of society's expectations of them as men and women. In the process, they become more aware not only of their own individuality, but also of the needs and feelings of others. Indeed, a child's increasing ability to function successfully in the world is one of the major accomplishments of these formative years.

Changing Relationships in a Larger Community

As the world of your school-age child expands to include a wider circle of individuals and a broader range of experiences, he will begin to see himself as a member of an ever-enlarging community. The insulated, self-centeredness of early childhood will fade and be replaced by a new, more mature self-awareness. You may find some aspects of his changing self-image wonderful, others frustrating, and still others unsettling and worrisome. It is perfectly normal for a child to both cling to a parent and pull away at the same time. Be sensitive to this conflict. And since every youngster matures at a different rate, it is important that you neither rush nor limit him. Instead, help your child to develop at a pace that suits his own unique personality and emerging social skills.

Your child's changing self-image

As your six-year-old becomes more and more involved with the people around him, he will begin comparing himself to them. He will react to these comparisons with pride and self-confidence perhaps, in one instance, embarrassment or feelings of inadequacy in another. As your youngster grows older still, the opinions of others will play an even greater role in shaping his sense of worth. And he will become even more reliant on his peers as reinforcers and models of appropriate behavior—and sometimes of inappropriate behavior as well.

The parent's shifting role

With your child's emerging independence, your parenting style will likely change too. Instead of the almost exclusive influence in her life, you will find yourself being more of a guide to her. Though no longer the sole agent in her socialization, you will still be instrumental to the process and should strive to be removed enough to allow growth, yet close enough to direct and nurture it. Through continuing identification with you and imitation of your behavior, your youngster will pick up many of your attitudes and values, and she will adopt them as her own.

Maintaining communication

As with all relationships, a parent-child bond thrives on openness. Talking with and listening closely to your young one is vital *(box, page 65)*. Maintaining early childhood rituals will also help you keep communication lines open. The fact that your child is growing up is no reason to end her storytime with you; as she learns to read, you can take turns reading out loud to each other. And now, more than ever, mealtimes and joint television-viewing can be forums for fruitful family discussions.

Before a crowd of parents and siblings, a young batter receives instructions from the coach in a teeball game. Organized sports present opportunities for children to interact and learn new skills, while giving parents the chance to remain involved in their youngsters' expanding universe.

Gender identification Even as your child sees herself and you in a new light, she is studying society as a whole, learning the subtle nuances of gender, and becoming aware of their implications. Whereas a four-year-old may take the whimsical view that clothes or hair style define masculinity and femininity, not so the first-grader. Having grappled with her gender identity—her essential biological femaleness—a six-year-old may now announce: "When I grow up, I'm going to be a mommy." This youngster is now in the process of refining her gender role by adapting what she believes to be the personality traits, interests, and behavior patterns of her sex. Another little girl, exposed to different standards in the family setting, might as easily say, "When I grow up, I'm going to be a doctor."

Imitation of adult gender-role models is an easy way for girls and boys in middle childhood to learn and adopt the traits that are associated with their sex. Their identification is further reinforced by the behavior of their peers and others in the society at large. For the most part, parents—especially those of the same sex as the child—are the models whose behavior the child generally imitates most closely.

But today, when an ever-growing number of children live in one-parent households at some point in their lives, having access to the parent of the same gender may not always be possible. If this is your family situation, you should make an extra effort to ensure that your youngster has opportunities to develop close relationships with a scout leader, a coach, a relative, or a family friend who might serve as a surrogate. It does not matter that the relationship lacks the intensity of a normal father-son or mother-daughter affiliation. The important thing is that the youngster has access to a suitable person after whom she can pattern some of her own behavior.

During this period, your child will come to see that in the eyes of many people, certain toys and activities are regarded as being sex appropriate. In this more restricted view, for example, only girls can play with dolls, and boys with trucks. But if there are general standards for sex-appropriate behavior, it is up to you,

This handwritten thank-you note from a seven-year-old to his father includes an intricately drawn maze, made by the boy as a token of gratitude. Such free and open communication is a sign of a warm and loving parent-child relationship.

as a parent, to enforce them or discard them as you see fit. Some parents may try to eliminate stereotypical gender roles by inviting a daughter to pitch in on a home repair project and encouraging a son to lend a hand with the household cooking and cleaning. Other parents may follow a more traditional path by making greater demands on a son in an attempt to prod him toward independence, while fostering a daughter's continued dependence on them.

Fathers and sex-role identification For reasons the experts do not fully understand, fathers, even more than mothers, affect their children's development of sex roles. Research indicates that children with fathers who are highly involved in rearing them are characterized by greater empathy and a stronger sense of their own potency than children with fathers who back off from the opportunity, leaving child care to their wives.

A father can be as positive a role model for a daughter as he can for a son. He can help his daughter develop confidence and determination by taking her accomplishments seriously and by not being afraid to discipline her when necessary. There is also a great deal of evidence to support the notion that girls who identify partly with their fathers turn out to be women with high self-esteem and the ability to act independently. Furthermore, the quality of a daughter's relationship with her father, the first man in her life, can to a large extent set the tone for her future relationships with men.

Talking Effectively with Your Child

Open and honest communication with your child is fundamental to being a good parent. But not all parents know how to communicate effectively with their children. Here are some pointers for improving understanding:

Make a commitment to talking with your child. Pick out a fixed time for a discussion, such as her bedtime. If you feel spontaneity is important, look for an occasion to strike up a conversation, while driving her, say, to a girl scout meeting, or cleaning up after dinner. Or come up with an event, such as having lunch together in a restaurant. Show your youngster that you are genuinely interested in talking with her.

And when conversing, give your child your full respect, using language that she can comprehend. Talk seriously about the things she feels are important. Matters you think are minor she may see as

major, and your willingness to listen to all of her concerns will encourage her to continue to share them with you as she grows older.

If beginning a conversation is awkward, try easing into it with a little humor. The experience of sharing real laughter can help you and your child feel more deeply connected. At first it might be wise to minimize direct personal questions, which can put your child on guard. Perhaps begin by talking about something that interests you both. Share experiences with each other.

Listening is as important a part of communicating as talking. When you listen, listen aggressively. Show your youngster the same respect you want in return. Look at her directly and maintain eye contact. Listen until she is finished talking; do not interrupt even if you see flaws in her logic or feel you have to

make a point. Let her know you have heard her by repeating what she said in your own words, or ask questions for clarification. Children are still mastering the nuances of language, and it is important that you and your child understand each other right from the beginning.

Not only do you have to be able to listen to what your child is saying, you must also be sensitive to the unspoken signals, to know when her behavior, attitude, or even facial expression is conveying more than her words.

Real communication can be difficult to maintain as your youngster moves through middle childhood. At times it may seem that the lines are closed. Persist. If you have laid the groundwork effectively, you can be certain that communication will in fact go on, and never will it count for more than in the years of adolescence that lie ahead.

The effect of working mothers

In today's world, a mother may often work outside the home. It is only natural for parents to worry about the potentially adverse effects a mother's absence may have on the development of a child. Reassuringly, studies indicate that in the area of gender indentification the children of working mothers are more apt to see sex roles in an egalitarian light and are less likely to view their parents in strictly stereotypical terms. Moreover, the same research shows that the daughters of working women are often highly motivated achievers who do well both in school and in their careers and tend to associate a woman's role in life with freedom of choice, satisfaction, and competence. For their part, the sons of working women tend to view women as more competent and men as warmer and more capable of free self-expression than do the sons of mothers who do not work outside the home.

Some mothers deliberately choose to work as fulltime homemakers in order to be more involved with their children's day-to-day development and to offer direct love and support, espe-

At an after-school recreation program, one girl waltzes with the adult monitor while three other youngsters kick up their heels to the music. Many public schools offer such programs as a service to families in which both the mother and father work outside the home.

When Children Must Cope on Their Own

Families with two working parents or those headed by a single parent who is also the breadwinner have become increasingly commonplace. As a result, many children are left unattended after school unless an alternate solution can be found. Some parents fall back on day-care centers or help from relatives, housekeepers, neighbors, or sitters. Others are able to work part-time, have flexible hours, or job share. Many people, however, must count on their youngsters to fend for themselves.

How well these so-called latchkey children cope depends on their level of maturity and on how their parents prepare them. Some eight-year-olds might be ready for such a step, while other youngsters might not be ready until they are fourteen or so. Left by herself at home, a child may experience boredom, loneliness, and fear, and if her parents can allay these feelings realistically, she can gain confidence and take pride in her new responsibilities.

Keeping an open line of communication between the parents and child is vital. From the outset, a youngster needs to know why a parent who used to be home is now going off to work. She should be included in planning her after-school routine. She should also be told exactly what is expected of her; a list of do's and don'ts and notes or daily tape-recorded messages with instructions for various chores will provide direction and keep her busy.

Watching television, pursuing a hobby, or cuddling a pet may ease the loneliness. A dog, especially, offers companionship, affection, and a feeling of security. Chatting with friends on the telephone also helps pass the time.

Safety, of course, must be a major concern. Many parents have their child call them upon arriving home from school. Leaving numbers and names to contact in case of emergencies is a must. Parents should also provide a basic first-aid kit and show their child how to use it, and they should conduct periodic fire drills. Additionally, they should tell a child never to let anyone know she is alone without first having obtained parental approval to do so, and never to open the door to strangers or to enter the house if there is a broken window or an unlocked door, or an unknown car in the driveway. If a youngster is at home when someone tries to break in, she should slip outside, go to a neighbor's house, and call the police.

Finally, parents should maintain an atmosphere of mutual trust and periodically praise their child for her responsible and mature behavior.

cially during the formative years of growing up. These mothers can, of course, instill nonstereotypical attitudes in their children through deliberate effort.

Encouraging independence

At every opportunity, nudge your school-age child along the path to independence, remaining near enough to monitor her progress while providing room enough for her to venture into new relationships on her own. Children need the freedom to try new things. Only you can know when you are pushing too hard and when you are hanging on too tightly.

A successful executive, recalling her childhood, remembered wanting to climb a particularly tall tree. Her mother, afraid that her daughter might fall, tried to hold her back, but her father gave the go-ahead. "My dad said that if I fell, I would learn a good lesson about what my limits were," she remembers, "but if I made it, I'd learn not to always let others set limitations for me. I climbed that tall tree right to the top and I can tell you I never forgot that lesson."

Building a relationship with others

Now is the time to encourage your child to reach out to people outside the immediate family. Not all youngsters are eager to make new friends. A few, especially only children who have grown used to their parents' companionship, may feel no great need to branch out. But flattering as your child's devotion to you might be, it serves only to stunt his social growth. By the beginning of puberty, almost all children will have become totally engrossed in their peer culture. An early start on socialization will help your child prepare for the turbulent teenage years that lie ahead, when personal stability can make all the difference to his future. ∴

The Importance of Friends

Beginning in the first grade, your child's playmates will assume greater prominence in his life, and making friends will become a major focus of his attention. Although sometimes short-lived, the ensuing relationships play an essential part in your youngster's social development.

Why having friends matters

Friends, or the lack of them, can have a profound effect on your youngster's current—and future—happiness. More than mere partners in play, friends are a principal means by which a child learns how to get along with others. Through friends, children develop essential interpersonal skills, such as the capacity to give and receive confidences, to avoid or resolve conflicts amicably, and to rely on and trust others.

Developing the ability to become part of a group may be even more important than learning how to form and maintain a one-on-one relationship. Studies indicate that children who are unable to get close to other children, or who are shunned and excluded by their peers, are likely to be lonely and to dislike school since it is such an unpleasant place to be. As a result, they may lose interest and begin to fail in their subjects. Furthermore, when these lonely children grow older they are likely to drop out of school, become juvenile delinquents, or suffer far more emotional adjustment problems than their classmates who had many friendships.

Three stages of childhood friendships

At some time or other, nearly every parent worries about his child's ability to make friends. Yet making friends can be learned. Your awareness of the various stages that elementary-school children go through in forming friendships will help you see better where your child stands in regard to this important developmental skill. If your ten-year-old is having difficulty making friends, perhaps it is because he is still using friendship-making techniques that worked when he was five years old but that other children have outgrown.

For children between the ages of six and eight, friendship is basically a one-way relationship—a friend being someone who does something for someone else. When asked why he plays with a certain child, a youngster may reply: "Because he likes to play a lot," or "Because he lets me use his toy soldiers." But as the process of socialization continues, the possibility of forging deeper friendships emerges. From the ages of nine through eleven, children begin to develop more of a qualitative and reciprocal viewpoint, making friends with children with whom they have certain things in common, such as physical appear-

ance, athletic interests, or musical abilities, and with whom they can have a give-and-take relationship. Starting around the age of twelve, their friendships take on a more adult quality. Youngsters begin to share thoughts and emotions, show concern for each other, and adhere to the same value system.

How to make friends For some children, making friends does not come naturally at all. But there are ways to help. First of all, when a child has no friends and shows little interest in making friends, the real reason may be that she does not know how. And here you can be of assistance by offering some direct coaching in how to approach other children and maintain the friendships that are formed. You might ask your child what kind of games her classmates like to play and probe to make sure that she has an adequate understanding of the rules. If an important ingredient to being accepted involves mastering certain skills, such as dancing, jumping rope, or kicking a ball, practice with her at home.

One important component of friendships among children is, of course, the sharing of common interests and viewpoints. Encourage your youngster to look for similarities between herself and others, and give her suggestions for using these to initiate conversations. Coach her to avoid coercive or argumentative behavior. Emphasize the importance of taking turns and sharing, and help her learn the art of compromise. Stress the value of listening carefully and responding. One of the more important skills that your child can learn is to recognize other children's feelings and desires.

Sometimes, in the wake of repeated rejection, children begin to fear that they are unworthy—perhaps because they are overweight or poorly coordinated. But all children have positive qualities. You can help a child suffering from low self-esteem feel better by pointing out the attributes that make her special. Let her know that everybody is excluded from one group or another at some time during childhood; it is a part of growing up. Help her see beyond the momentary rejection. You might even cite your own childhood experience in this area.

You and your child's friends

Allowing your child to choose his friends is an important factor in helping him grow up. But you will want to know whom he has chosen; it will tell you much about how he is developing and the day-to-day influences and pressures that he faces.

Not all of his friends may be to your liking, but as long as a particular friendship is not destructive or dangerous, try not to interfere. Resist any urge to judge his friends solely by your standards. If his companions are unsuitable, he will realize that eventually. By challenging his choice, you may only motivate him to defend the friendship and keep it going longer than it otherwise might last. If you are concerned about the quality of his friends, there are ways for you to keep abreast of those friendships and perhaps steer him toward more fruitful relationships. You might suggest a group excursion and then serve as chaperone, or arrange for your child to spend some time with a youngster you wish he would get to know better. (Perhaps a friendship will grow out of the exposure—but again, do not force the issue.) Or you could encourage him to invite some children he likes home so they can have fun and you can get to know them better. It is important that he realize you care about his companions and that you will support him and help him in forming and preserving friendships as best you can. ∴

Boys and Girls Together

As boys and girls figure out their gender identities, their attitude toward each other changes. Whereas two youngsters may have played side by side in complete harmony as toddlers, now a powerful sense of identification with being male or female pulls them apart, and both of them show a strong preference for playmates of the same sex. This developmental phase, which is referred to by child psychologists as sex cleavage, is a normal and healthy part of growing up and usually continues to the onset of puberty.

The causes of sex cleavage

The desire of boys to play with boys, and girls to play with girls, during the middle childhood years is deeply rooted and occurs in countries all over the world. Such behavior lends support to the theories of some experts that children are biologically programmed for initial cleavage. Cultural influences, of course, also play a major role in reinforcing the separation of the sexes by expecting—indeed, often demanding—stereotypical behavior of each. And the gap is further widened by the emergence of increasingly dissimilar interests.

The importance of boys and girls playing together

When growing boys and girls have opportunities to interact with one another, like the children working together on a sand sculpture below, important groundwork is laid for the development of healthy relationships with the opposite sex later on in life. In addition, closer contact between the sexes at this age helps foster the kind of mutual respect that can provide a smoother

transition into adolescence. And this will be especially true if parents encourage and facilitate such encounters on a natural and convenient basis.

Encouraging mutuality
You can promote better understanding on the part of your youngster by turning a deaf ear to her avowals that she "hates" boys or that all boys are "dumb." Help her, instead, to seek out common ground on which she can play with boys on equal terms, perhaps by providing opportunities for her to participate with them in mutually pleasing sports, such as teeball or soccer. You might also invite friends of yours who have a child of the opposite sex but the same age as your own youngster to come to your home, or plan family gatherings that give boy and girl cousins the chance to play together and get to know one another better. Such contacts, even when they are kept up fairly regularly, may not blossom into full-blown friendships, but they will accustom your child to the idea of spending time with members of the opposite sex. You might see to it, too, that stereotypical attitudes are not being perpetuated in the milieu of your youngster's classroom. Studies have shown that teachers who make an effort to downplay sex-typing and upgrade cooperation between boys and girls see their efforts rewarded by a significant increase in play between them.

Boys together
The often self-imposed segregation of the sexes in middle childhood is further reflected in the different play patterns of boys and girls, especially in the way in which each sex goes about forming peer groups. Whereas boys tend to align themselves in relatively large groups of four to eight, girls customarily form two-person friendships. Given their larger size, boys' groups are usually less exclusive than those formed by girls, operating on a kind of open-door policy that results in a constantly changing cast of characters.

At some point, eight- to twelve-year-old boys may flaunt the rules of adult society and engage in such antisocial but typically boyish pranks as ringing doorbells or surreptitiously removing a For Sale sign and placing it on an unwitting neighbor's lawn. Experts point out that being part of a group is important to a boy's development, as it provides him with solidarity and support in his search for his own identity. Typically in such situations, it is always "we" who turns out to have performed the rebellious exploit and never "I." Boys are also far more apt to have peer-group conflicts and fight with one another than girls are. These behavior patterns are mirrored in the games the sexes

Male and Female: An Artful Difference

Girls and boys in the middle childhood years are both struggling to discover and define who they are—and this shows up in their art. And because they are not ready to express gender identification subtly, they gravitate to those symbols that are immediately associated with being male or female in our culture.

Boys seem preoccupied with monsters, dinosaurs, superheroes, and other subjects of a combative nature, and their pictures are characteristically full of motion and complex interactions *(right)*. War and battle scenes, often including hordes of men, ground equipment, and planes; sports events; factories; and space launchings emerge as popular images.

Girls tend to focus on themes related to individuals and interpersonal relationships. They reveal a clear preference for flowers, trees, and houses. Girls also make pictures of people of all ages, including babies and glamorous teenagers, and draw both sexes, whereas boys are more apt to depict the male only. And many girls, particularly as they reach the mid-elementary-school years, become enamored of horses and explore this theme with intensity, even when they have had little or no experience with the animals *(below)*.

Sometimes boys and girls cross over in their artwork. For a boy to draw horses, and a girl space launchings, is no more a sign of gender confusion than the destructiveness so often depicted in boys' art is a sign of a dangerously violent nature. These subjects serve children well in their expression of gender awareness, and it is in the child's best interests that he be allowed to explore his ideas without too much interference. As children mature and develop, they will abandon these themes and move on to new subject matter more socially acceptable in nature.

Sylvia G. Feinburg, Ed.D.
Associate Professor, Eliot-Pearson Department of Child Study
Tufts University, Medford, Massachusetts

prefer. Boys tend to like those activities that require a relatively large number of players and strenuous physical exertion, as opposed to jumping rope, playing house, and other so-called girls' games, which are often less vigorous and are more suited to two-person friendships.

Girls together　If boys are the free-spirited group animal of middle childhood, then girls are the personification of loyalty. Girls are more selective in their choice of friends, preferring to link up in pairs of best friends, an inclination that is strengthened by society's reinforcement of the image of girls as being quieter, calmer, less aggressive, and more nurturing than boys.

Whereas a boy might think of a friend as "an ally in open rebellion," as psychologists Joseph Adelson and Elizabeth Douvan have put it, a girl sees her best friend as a confidant to whom she can entrust her innermost thoughts and feelings. According to Adelson and Douvan, she views friendship as "a source of support and a repository of confidences." Thus, girls tell each other secrets, write confidential notes to each other, talk about relationships, and show affection openly by hugging and holding hands. Perhaps because of cultural taboos against female aggression, girls rarely fight, and when they do they generally use words instead of fists. They also tend to forbear boys' harassment without resorting to physical violence.

With girls' friendships founded in intimacy, it is not surprising that their relationships are more restrictive, or that jealousy can sometimes be a make-or-break factor in them. Some two-girl friendships expand into trios, but for the most part, pairs of girls, like links in a chain, may forge themselves into a clique that depends on its member pairs for strength.

The first stirrings of romance　The studied aversion of boys for girls, and girls for boys, usually comes to an end sometime during the fifth- or sixth-grade years, opening the way for the emergence of heterosexual interests in early adolescence. But the patterns of behavior are usually still strained, amounting to little more than sidelong glances, schoolyard teasing, and hastily denied rumors of "who likes who." At the first sign of overt affection, both boy and girl are likely to beat a retreat to the safety of their respective peer groups where same-sex friends can provide advice and encouragement or the matter can be conveniently dropped or forgotten. Nevertheless, it is upon such tentative encounters as these that the deeper romantic attachments of the teenage and adult years eventually come to be built. ❖

Coping with Conflict

Conflicts are inevitable among growing children. But just as youngsters learn how to argue and fight, so too must they learn how to resolve their disputes without resorting to aggressive behavior. Every child needs to be taught the importance of controlling his temper and the value of compromise.

Rough-and-tumble play

Not all fighting is real fighting. Many children, especially boys, enjoy chasing each other about, jumping on top of each other, and wrestling. What separates this pretend fighting from the real thing is that the players are friends and their aggressive actions are usually accompanied by smiles and giggles.

The nature of fighting and aggression

Knowing how to handle conflicts begins with an understanding of the nature of aggression and how it finds outlets. To some experts, aggression can be categorized as being either hostile or, as they put it, instrumental. Hostile aggression is marked by the child's intent to hurt someone else in retaliation for actions that angered, threatened, or frustrated him. Boys and girls who strike out like this often see the world as more threatening than it is. They misinterpret the actions of others and presume hostility where none exists. These children must somehow learn that the world is not as threatening as it seems.

Instrumental aggression occurs when the child has not been provoked but simply wants to take something, such as another child's toy. Once he succeeds in getting his way through force, he resorts to it again, and then again, until the pattern becomes ingrained.

Children who employ either of these behaviors are usually unskilled at making friends, and other children dislike them. As a parent, you should tolerate neither form of behavior from your child. Instead, encourage the youngster to find more acceptable outlets

The grins on their faces indicate clearly that these boys are not angry with each other, but enjoying a friendly wrestling match. Such rough-and-tumble play, essential to development, can sometimes lead to real fighting if one child misinterprets the physical actions of the other.

for his feelings; if need be, you may have to turn to professionals for assistance with the problem.

Learning aggression   Children often model their aggressive behavior after peers, friends, siblings, television shows, parents, and other adults. Indiscriminate viewing of television violence is much more likely to lead to aggressive behavior than the decreased exposure that occurs when parents monitor shows. And even a nonaggressive youngster can learn to behave aggressively, if after being victimized he then responds by adopting the behavior of the aggressor.

Sometimes, well-meaning parents can unwittingly cater to and reinforce a child's aggressive tendencies. They may give in to his tantrums or, proud of his aggression, may wrongly praise him for using force to get his way. Peers, too, can indulge a child's aggressive conduct by allowing it to succeed or by providing examples to copy. When a youngster sees a friend get away with bending the rules of a game to suit himself, for example, he may attempt to use the same tactic.

Parents of children prone to aggression can take comfort in knowing that what was learned can often be unlearned, especially if the tendencies are detected early. Undoing the damage consists of teaching a child socially accepted behaviors, such as cooperation and taking turns, and of making him aware of the consequences of his aggression.

Defusing arguments   The best way to handle a fight is to stay near enough to step in, so as to forestall injury or to nudge the parties toward negotiation, but to otherwise stay out of it. No matter how well-intentioned, a preemptive intervention by you only signals your willingness to ride to your child's rescue at the merest hint of trouble, rather than putting her and her peers on notice that they must learn how to resolve their own conflicts.

You can act as mediator by encouraging the parties involved to talk about what happened and why, and by making sure that everybody concerned listens to all sides of the argument. You can suggest solutions if you wish, but be sure to let the children themselves make the decisions. Ideally, they will be able to work out a solution that will be fair. Praise them for trying to reach an amicable settlement.

Dealing with bullies   Bullies are children who think that force works. According to psychologist Dan Olweus, they are a subset of aggressive children who enjoy hurting other children, physically or psycho-

Oh, Those Endless Squabbles

❝ Before meals my children seem to be at their most vulnerable. Arguments escalate quickly. Usually the kids work it out themselves, but when the bickering goes on too long, I send them to their bedrooms for a time out. Once they've cooled off, it's as though nothing was ever wrong. ❞

❝ Playing with others has become more of a problem than it was when my two boys were little. Tommy is ten now and has many friends. If Mike, who is seven, wants to tag along, he can usually worm his way in. But when Tommy wants to be part of Mike's circle, he tends to act the boss, and that doesn't go over well with the younger kids. Sometimes Mike will blow up and tell Tommy to go find his own friends. If that doesn't work, Mike comes to me. I explain to Tommy that Mike wants to play alone with his friends and suggest alternative activities to Tommy. ❞

❝ My kids occasionally struggle with each other. Recently Susan was playing quietly when Andrew came home from school. Instead of asking whether he could play with her, he just grabbed her doll. She, of course, tried to get it back. My son, delighted to have her attention, continued to hold the doll out of reach. When episodes like this happen, I usually get them to talk about what happened and why. Fortunately, they've never been jealous of each other, and things soon calm down. ❞

❝ My sons are very conscious of rules, especially when it comes to playing games, and if one departs from the rules, an argument is not far off. Sometimes they will agree upon a change almost instantly. Other times neither is willing to give in. And even though it can be annoying to listen to them thrash it out, that's what I try to do. They rarely fight, but when an argument turns to blows I separate them and solicit at least a perfunctory apology. Then when they've cooled off, I help the two of them work out an acceptable solution. ❞

❝ In our house there is a comfortable couch in the TV room, positioned for the best viewing. In the evening, when the kids head in to watch their favorite shows, they can start out sharing the couch harmoniously. But as the night wears on they both want to stretch out a little more, get a little more comfortable, put their feet in each other's way, and so on. When I hear them start to raise their voices and accuse each other of "Crossing over to my side!" I know it's time to step in. A few routine questions—who was here first, who had the couch last night, who got to choose the show—are usually enough to remind them that they have to reach a compromise, and they do. ❞

❝ Halloween wouldn't be Halloween around our house without The Fight. William collects as much candy as possible, and takes inventory before socking it all away. Jane, who is a bit older, is more interested in roaming with her

friends than in trick-or-treating. Once she has exhausted her supply of candy, she digs into William's. He notices and the name-calling and yelling start, escalating pretty steadily until I put a stop to it. Every year I explain to Jane that it's wrong to take William's candy, and without fail the scene is repeated the following year. Maybe next year . . . ❞

logically, simply for the fun of it. Aggression is a way of life to them, and they rarely pick a fair fight. Sooner or later, your youngster is likely to have a run-in with one.

What makes a bully? Most researchers blame poor parental influence. As Olweus says, "Too little love and care and too much freedom in childhood contribute strongly to the development of an aggressive personality." Or a bully can be the product of a parent who chooses criticism and sarcasm over encouragement as a way of dealing with a child, and who often resorts to physical punishment. Given their unsociable attributes, it is not surprising that bullies have few friends. More disturbing is the fact that most bullies never do outgrow their aggressiveness and thus face grim prospects as adults. Studies of eight-year-old male bullies have shown that they have a four to five times greater chance of having a criminal record by the age of thirty than do normal boys of the same age.

Handling a bully is a thorny problem. Merely informing him that his aggressive behavior is wrong rarely works, since to a bully just about any act of aggression can be justified. If your child exhibits a need to pick on others, intervene immediately. Tell him in no uncertain terms that such behavior will not be tolerated. And back up your words with some form of nonphysical punishment, such as making him sit by himself for a few minutes. Later, talk to him about his behavior and explain the effect such behavior has on other children. Find out what sparked his outburst. Your child may not know any other way of interacting, so you may well have to help him find alternative responses. A careful review of your own relationship with him is also in order. You will need to make sure that you are not modeling the very same behavior that you are trying to correct.

Helping the victim Searching for answers as to why they were singled out, the victims of bullies often feel alone in their unhappiness. Out of shame or fear, they may refuse to talk about the incident. Knowing when your child has been bullied often requires an awareness on your part of subtle changes in his attitude toward himself. Never minimize his concerns. As a parent, you need to hug him and reassure him that he is not a coward or a failure just because he has been victimized and that the bully alone was the one at fault. You can also give him some advice that may lessen the chances of a recurrence.

Experts generally recommend a series of escalating responses to deal with the problem, based on the idea that a child who does not respond as the bully desires is unlikely to be chosen as a target again. He should try to ignore his attacker's taunts, thus denying the bully the attention he craves. If that fails, he should stand up to the bully verbally by assuming an air of authority and ordering the bully to stop. The intended victim should then walk away from the situation. If the bully still persists and hits the child, the victim should feel free, as a last resort, to defend himself. The unexpected show of strength may stop the incident. Sometimes, however, it may be necessary to seek help from a teacher or other adult in authority. In the wake of such an encounter, reinforce your child's self-esteem by making him understand that he was not responsible for the bully's behavior and that it is the bully, not himself, who has a problem. •ː•

Who's In and Who's Out

During the middle childhood years, a youngster's need to belong to a group grows ever stronger, until by adolescence it can seem that there are few things that matter more to her than peer acceptance and approval. Indeed, for some children being in with the right crowd becomes the main focus of their lives and the most important reason for going to school.

The importance of the group

Inclusion in a peer group is a developmental rite of passage, one that reflects a child's growing desire for social acceptance as well as an increasing need for freedom from parental control. The dynamics of group interaction provide opportunities for a youngster not only to exercise new social skills, but also to come to terms with the ups and downs of inclusion and rejection. In the group, your child will gain a clearer sense of herself, as she compares her own personality and abilities with those of her friends. Her companions are even more important as models of behavior; it is almost inevitable that she will pick up certain traits and behaviors of theirs that she sees as successful.

Whether large or small, the peer group itself typically takes the form of a team or a clique. While boys commonly gather in large groups and girls in small ones composed of pairs of close

Clad in what amounts to a uniform, these eleven- and twelve-year-old boys follow a fad for colorful knee-length shorts. At an age when inclusion in the group is all-important, a little conformity, especially in the matter of clothing, can go a long way toward helping children fit in and feel part of a larger community.

79

friends, both often become intensely involved in establishing their own "official" clubs. The founding members will enthusiastically come up with a name for their organization, concoct a stew of membership requirements, devise rituals, choose officers, and award titles. They may even build a clubhouse from scavenged materials. Then, often within days, the group disbands, its momentum consumed. Even so, these short-lived clubs provide experience in organization, allowing children to make and break their own rules, test their leadership skills, and decide for themselves who should belong.

Sitting apart, a shy girl watches wistfully as three of her classmates share a note. All that usually separates a shy child from more outgoing peers are the social skills needed to bridge the gap, which can be learned and nurtured through parental encouragement and reinforcement.

Conformity Inclusion in a group almost always entails some degree of conformity. To your child, such matters as what kind of clothing to wear, what sort of bike to ride, and whether to buy lunch at school or bring it are a small price to pay for admission—even if it seems to you to entail loss of self-determination.

Indeed, a certain amount of conformity should be expected and even encouraged in a child. You may not approve of the group's dress code, for example, but it will not hurt your child to wear loud socks or a certain brand of sneakers. And it just may contribute to his sense of belonging. At the same time, you can help him see that there is more to being friends than wearing the latest fad. In the long run your child's unquestioning loyalty to a group, like his earlier blind devotion to family, will be just another step on the road to self-discovery and responsibility.

Peer pressure Like the desire to conform, peer pressure among children is the bane of many parents, and it will grow heavier as your child nears adolescence. But not all peer pressure is bad. When group energies are channeled into constructive activities, such as athletics or Scouting, it can promote the very values and behavioral

traits you are working to instill. Trouble starts when those who are in decide that the price of staying in requires socially unacceptable behavior. Withstanding that kind of pressure can be difficult, and your direct intervention may be needed. Prepare your child in advance, through coaching and role-playing, to face such situations, to make a worthwhile decision, and to stand by it confidently *(pages 102-107)*.

Every parent of a nine- to twelve-year-old is familiar with that great childhood rationalizer—namely, "Everybody." Ask your youngster why he must have those expensive sunglasses, and likely as not he will respond that "Everybody has them." The same Everybody also seems to get the biggest allowance and the best dirt bike, and can stay up as late as he wants. Likewise, Everybody can always be found at the movies your own child is not allowed to see. Invisible and seemingly invincible, Everybody is, of course, the soul of the group and a partner in your young one's search for an identity of his own outside the family. This form of peer pressure can grate, but you can take heart in knowing that it will wane as your child gains confidence.

Following the leader With confidence may come a desire to lead. Almost as soon as a group or club forms, one or more children will rise to the top. These leaders tend to be outgoing and energetic, witty and sociable, and they often have some specific skills needed by the group. In addition, the best group leaders are sensitive to the

How to Help a Shy Child Overcome Shyness

Most parents, quite naturally, want their child to feel as happy and welcome at school or on the playground as he is at home, so it is hard to say who suffers more when a youngster is shy: the parents or the youngster himself.

Shy children are different from quiet children, who by nature are truly content to go off by themselves to read or engage in other relatively solitary activities. And shy children are not necessarily rejected or left-out children, who lack the skills to make and maintain friendships. Their inhibition lies in making initial contact and entering groups, and happily, there are some things parents can do about it.

First, if your child is shy, avoid labeling him as such, because it can become a self-fulfilling prophecy. Sensing your anxiety, he is likely to become even more tense about interacting. Instead,

look for positive ways to shape his attitude. Expose him to a wide range of social experiences. Involve yourself, when appropriate, in your child's activities so that he will feel comfortable about participating in them. If he plays soccer, chauffeur the neighborhood athletes to the playing field, for example, or volunteer to host a meeting of his Scout troop. Having him join an after-school activity group or arranging visits with cousins or the children of family friends are other ways to accustom your child to being around many different kinds of youngsters his own age.

At the same time, however, it is best not to subject your child to the "sink or swim" approach of socializing; better that he be eased gradually into new situations. A shy youngster does not like to stand out in the crowd, so you can help him to fit in by allowing him to wear

clothes or a hair style that is in keeping with current fashion. Teach him a skill (even one that may seem trivial to you) that might be admired by the neighborhood boys and girls; and try to make your home or yard an inviting place for youngsters his age to be.

Most important, perhaps, concentrate on building your youngster's self-esteem, since experts believe that a poor self-image is responsible for many children's shyness. Besides complimenting him and letting him know you love him just as he is, try having him care for a pet or for a child a few years younger. This will boost his confidence by making him feel needed and important.

Finally, you should not ignore such things as rest, nutrition, and a peaceful home life: Studies have shown that energy and happiness are keys to popularity for people of all ages.

needs of the individual members of the group.

Being "in" Generally speaking, the children who are members of what the others consider the best group become the most popular youngsters in their community. They often share traits such as attractiveness and outgoing, cooperative personalities. Popular children are better at initiating play, negotiating conflicts, and working out acceptable solutions. They can be teased without getting angry, and they accept their own failures. They are also better at social problem-solving, display more empathy toward peers, and can more accurately assess the actions of others. Finally, popular children can anticipate the consequences of their own conduct.

And on the "out" Rejection is inevitable in child's play, and it happens to everybody at some time. To some children, however, rejection is such a constant companion that it adversely affects their social development. Besides their inability to enter groups, rejected children have similar behaviors—for the most part, the opposite of popular children's. Rejected children, for example, cannot settle conflicts without creating a winner and a loser. When teased,

Staying up late watching television and combing one another's hair, preteenage friends enjoy a slumber party at the home of one of the girls. Parents can help their child's social evolution by providing her with plenty of opportunities to participate in such healthy peer-group activities.

they get angry, and when they fail, they refuse to accept their shortcomings. Rejected children also cannot solve social problems, and they show less empathy. They frequently misinterpret the actions of others and cannot predict the consequences of their own deeds. If your youngster fits this pattern, you must deal with the problem now, so that he will not repeat the behavior later.

By the same token, there are children who are not in and are not considered rejected. They are proficient at making friends and are happy in their groups, even though they occupy a different position in their childhood society.

Shy and quiet children   Some children, including shy youngsters and those who are naturally quiet, never give a peer group a chance to accept or reject them. A shy child may want to belong, but cannot overcome her own shyness without help. Such youngsters often lack the skills of social competence. Quiet youngsters, on the other hand, get along easily with other children when they need to, but they really prefer their own company and interests to those of any group.

It is important, however, that all children learn to socialize. Otherwise, they risk carrying their truncated social skills into adolescence and adulthood. As a parent, you should take whatever steps are necessary to alleviate your child's reluctance to interact with others so that it does not become a social impediment to her *(box, page 81)*.

Helping your child belong   Your affectionate support will guide your youngster to social competence. Accept peer pressure as a fact of life, and encourage and help her to develop interpersonal skills: Provide plenty of opportunities for her to share the company of her friends. Sleepovers, parties, and group outings are all part of the fun of growing up, and you should make sure your child has time for them. By doing all you can to enhance her self-confidence and self-reliance, you make it easier for her to cut her own path in a world crowded with people. ⁘

Becoming a Good Citizen

A child's moral development is a weighty subject. No one agrees on exactly how to teach a youngster the difference between right and wrong, but most parents concur that a child's capacity to treat others with kindness, cooperation, and compassion must be actively cultivated. To guide a child from the egocentric cocoon of the preschool years to the more egalitarian world outside your home is a task of the first order.

The task is complicated by the fact that at the moment you would concentrate on teaching your child socially responsible behavior, he is at the age when he starts to realize that he lives in an imperfect world. On the heels of that recognition follows another revelation: Even parents make mistakes. Adult authority figures are not always right. This new knowledge on the child's part can be alarming to some parents, especially when it leads a youngster to ask with great intensity: "Why?"

Know, however, that recognizing adult fallibility can be valuable to a child, who needs to learn that failings of all kinds are only part of being human. While your child must have a strong model of positive social behavior to follow, admitting you are wrong now and then will help him to develop self-esteem based on realistic expectations of his own behavior. And just as the young crossing guards in the photograph opposite have discovered, your child will learn that making social contributions lies well within his reach.

The following pages offer a comprehensive view of how a school-age child develops judgment and good behavior. Teaching such behavior is admittedly a prickly task, since your youngster will be experiencing many competing demands on his life from peers, school, and the family itself; thus, emphasis is placed on helping him to develop methods for coping with the stressful challenges of middle childhood as he matures in his capacity to make wise decisions.

A Strengthening of Moral Fiber

No doubt you want your youngster to grow up to be a moral person and an upright citizen. Now, during these middle years of childhood, is the time when her moral development accelerates, unfolding with her quickening intellectual growth. As she improves her thinking and reasoning skills, she learns to make increasingly sophisticated judgments about right and wrong. As she gains new experiences and becomes better able to empathize—to put herself in someone else's place—she begins to base decisions about her behavior less on self-centered needs and more on her growing ability to understand and predict the feelings and reactions of others. Through school and neighborhood interactions with friends and classmates, she learns the value of cooperating and developing fair rules for play.

As a preschooler, your child understood the need to obey rules in order to avoid provoking your disapproval and to receive praise. She could also distinguish between rules that are based on moral principles—"No hitting your playmates"—and rules that are based on social convention: "No calling grownups by their first names." Such early childhood morality sets the stage for the more sophisticated moral reasoning of the elementary-school years.

Changing views of law and authority

At the start of middle childhood, most children define right and wrong in rigid, narrow terms. They accept rules and authority absolutely. While a preschooler or six- or seven-year-old may occasionally change a rule in the middle of a game, he will know that it is wrong to do so. An older child gradually understands that rules can be modified to deal with shifting circumstances. Accompanying this developing moral outlook is the emergence of the so-called golden rule mentality, which enables him to incorporate the rights of others into his moral thinking.

A simple two-stage theory of moral development

The influential child psychologist Jean Piaget suggested that children's moral development passes through two stages, moving from what he called a "morality of constraint" to a "morality of cooperation." In Piaget's first stage, a child views all laws, from the rules of a card game to parental rules for behavior, as inflexible, unchanging laws of nature. The concept of unjust laws or unfair use of authority is not part of the youngster's world view at this stage in his thinking. He does not take extenuating circumstances into account when making his moral judgments,

As their game of marbles gets under way, three boys discuss the rules so that they can play together without friction. Once older children like these know that rules exist for their mutual benefit, they eagerly master fair play.

and he believes that actions should be judged solely by their effects, not by the intentions behind them. When his desires conflict with an authority's rules, the child may try to fulfill them illicitly, sneaking the cookie, rather than asking whether he might have it. But if caught with the cookie in hand, he will typically accept punishment since he continues to believe that the authority is always right.

As the youngster progresses to Piaget's second stage and brings increasing cognitive maturity to bear on questions of right and wrong, he modifies his earlier views. He no longer regards rules as something carved in stone but perceives them as social arrangements subject to negotiation and change by group consent. This new view of cooperative group authority may be accompanied by an increased willingness to abide by the agreed-upon rules. His moral judgments now begin to take account of people's motives and intentions as well as the outcome of their actions. For instance, in the initial stage of moral development, the child would probably have said that a boy who breaks ten glasses is naughtier than a boy who breaks only one, even if the first boy drops a tray of dishes while helping his parents in the kitchen, and the second boy knocks over his single glass while climbing on a forbidden counter to raid the cookie jar. But in the second stage of moral development, weighing motives, the child would say that the cookie thief was naughtier, even though he did less damage, because he was trying to steal while the other boy was trying to be helpful.

Psychologists who have studied children's morality since Piaget have come to believe that his two-stage

model oversimplifies the complex process of moral development. One prominent researcher, Lawrence Kohlberg, has proposed a more comprehensive model that encompasses five stages. Kohlberg developed his five-stage theory by categorizing the answers given by people of different ages to hypothetical moral dilemmas, such as "Would it be right or wrong for a poor man to save his dying wife by stealing some expensive medicine from a rich druggist?"

In Kohlberg's first stage, a youngster's idea of doing right is a simple matter of obeying rules in order to avoid punishment and to get approbation. In the second stage, she learns to think in terms of fair exchanges and give-and-take. Good behavior now means fulfilling her own needs and desires while allowing others to do likewise. Obeying parents and other authority figures is no longer an automatic response to superior power, but an expression of the child's awareness that in exchange for obedience she will continue to receive guidance, nurturance, and other benefits. Through both of these stages, the youngster is thinking and reasoning in an egocentric fashion—the belief that she is the center of her own little universe. In the second stage she begins to understand that by being good, others will be good to her in turn, but her moral judgments still center on herself and the people with whom she has immediate interaction.

Although many children remain at stage two throughout middle childhood, some youngsters begin to show signs of stage-three thinking as they approach adolescence. This phase is characterized by conformity to what is regarded as good behavior and a desire to be seen by others as a good person. And since, in the child's mind, intentions are often more important than actual results, he is likely to respond to being caught in a transgression with "I didn't mean to do it," as though this alone were enough to excuse the act.

Stage four is marked by the child's ability to think of larger social needs, and by his devotion to duty and social order. Simply not meaning to have done something is no longer an acceptable excuse for him, especially, say, if by his act he has harmed someone. This stage is more likely to be achieved in late adolescence or early adulthood, if even then.

Moral thinking beyond childhood   Kohlberg's fifth stage involves a high level of abstract moral reasoning, well beyond the reach of elementary-school children, who lack the cognitive skills to make moral decisions at this complex level of thought. Judgments are now guided by a concern for individual rights, as well as respect for the social contract, society's agreement to use its laws for the greatest good for the greatest number.

Kohlberg at one time hypothesized a sixth stage in which people base their moral decisions on universal principles that may require them to depart from society's rules, as in the case of Martin Luther King, Jr., who engaged in civil disobedience to protest unjust, racist laws. But Kohlberg's research failed to find a significant enough sample of people operating at this level of moral reasoning for him to include it.

The bumpy path to behaving well

The five developmental stages in Kohlberg's model are not hard and fast categories. Your child does not jump from one stage to the next; he may even act inconsistently from situation to situation. You may find, for instance, that he reasons at a high level regarding one issue but cannot seem to get beyond stage one on another issue. Consider the youngster who spends all day helping out at the church fund-raiser for the poor and then comes home and unfairly blames his brother for messing up their bedroom, denying his own contributions to the disorder. This changeability can be exasperating for a parent, but it is a normal part of growing up.

Peer and parental influences on moral development

Your child's moral development owes a great debt to his emerging intellectual skills; no less vital, however, is his exposure to other children at school and in play situations. Learning how to cooperate with peers in games and other group activities teaches him to curb his egocentric needs, and he begins to establish relationships based on reciprocity and consideration for the feelings of others. Previously he has obeyed rules handed down by adult authority figures; now he finds himself on equal footing with his peers and in the gratifying position to develop rules for group behavior that result in equitable exchanges. Play helps along this essential process whereby your child abandons his earlier moral code based on self-gratification and avoidance of punishment and adopts a more sophisticated code based on fairness and mutual satisfaction.

Your child will benefit from hearing you, his teachers, and other important adults in his life discuss moral problems. Studies have shown that children who listen to adults engaged in a sophisticated discussion of moral issues respond with advances in their own moral reasoning. As your child sees you apply moral values to daily decisions, you will have a greater likelihood of success in communicating important values to her and preparing her to make wise moral judgments on her own. ∴

Lessons in Good Behavior

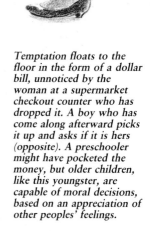

As your child's moral reasoning matures through middle childhood, does her behavior show the same moral progress? The two do not necessarily go together, and it should come as no surprise that her spontaneous behavior will not always keep pace with her moral reasoning. Adults, of course, are capable of highly sophisticated moral reasoning—and of cruelty, dishonesty, and numerous other vices at the same time. Clearly, moral behavior requires more than high-level cognitive skills and the ability to draw sophisticated conclusions about right and wrong.

Other influences on moral behavior

Knowing right from wrong is the first necessity for behaving morally, but knowledge by itself is not enough. It is one thing for a young child to make reasoned judgments when asked about the right course of action but something else altogether to know always how to monitor and control his own behavior amid the hurly-burly of the classroom, school playground, or the neighborhood turf. A school-age youngster's behavior is shaped by many factors, including the behavior of role models, consistent discipline with reasonable punishments and rewards, moral guidance from parents and teachers, and his own newfound ability to take someone else's perspective.

Despite your continuing influence, your direct authority—especially outside the home—will tend to fade in importance as your child reaches the end of middle childhood and as his social interactions with other children grow. At this stage, peers become an ever more powerful influence on a youngster's attitudes and behavior. In one study, researchers found that when questioned about behavior approved by their mothers and fathers but disapproved by their peers, children of this age sided with their parents less than one-third of the time. So the moral values of close friends will inevitably compete with the values that are taught at home.

Temptation floats to the floor in the form of a dollar bill, unnoticed by the woman at a supermarket checkout counter who has dropped it. A boy who has come along afterward picks it up and asks if it is hers (opposite). A preschooler might have pocketed the money, but older children, like this youngster, are capable of moral decisions, based on an appreciation of other peoples' feelings.

The value of self-control

In order to exhibit moral behavior, your child must learn to control and discipline herself. In infancy, when she demanded quick gratification of a few basic desires, self-control was an unknown concept. In early childhood, her control of her own behavior was still shaky, and she relied on firm adult guidance. Now in middle childhood, as she develops more mature thought processes, she acquires the ability to control her desires, defer gratification, and hold in mind a fairly consistent idea of right and wrong. If she is saving money for a special toy, for example, she must have the self-control to wait until she has accumulated enough to buy it, rather than squander her weekly allowance on candy. But even the most well-behaved youngster needs encouragement and praise to arrive at this new level of restraint. Remember that you will not always be there at your child's side when she has to make moral decisions, and thus your reinforcement of her efforts will matter a great deal.

Techniques for mastering self-control

Psychologists have identified a number of self-control strategies that you may wish to teach your youngster to help him in the normal childhood struggle to resist temptation, overcome distractions, and deal with other conflictual behavior issues.

Studies have shown that young children who are attempting a task requiring will are able to concentrate more successfully and keep from being sidetracked if they repeat to themselves, "I'm not going to look at it," or some other similar instruction.

Older children can use a more advanced technique to help themselves concentrate on what they are supposed to be doing. A group of sixth-grade math students, for instance, performed better on schoolwork than another group when each student monitored his own study behavior and recorded every instance of taking time out, and then used his self-monitoring as a reminder to get back to the lesson at hand.

Distraction is a useful technique for dealing with temptation. When your child was a preschooler, you probably found that you could easily turn his thoughts away from inappropriate behavior by diverting him with a toy, game, or story. As your child becomes older, you can encourage him to distract himself by deliberately turning his attention elsewhere when he finds himself faced with a temptation.

Enabling your child to become responsible

Although middle childhood is a period of increasing self-control for your youngster, your active discipline remains an important part of her moral growth. Ideally, your efforts to discipline your child will teach her how to make responsible decisions for herself. Since you will not always be on hand to impose external authority on her activities, it is important that you give your youngster help in developing her own internal moral authority, her own conscience.

Your choice of disciplinary techniques will have a definite effect on your child's ability to make independent judgments and to distinguish for herself between appropriate and inappropriate courses of action. According to experts, discipline styles fall into three broad categories—authoritarian, authoritative, and permissive. Authoritarian parents exert a good deal of control over their child's behavior, relying on their strength as an external authority figure; questions are discouraged. Authoritative parents tend to give the child firm guidelines for behavior but explain the reasons behind them; they also encourage give-and-take. Permissive parents set few limits to a youngster's behavior; it may be up to the child to decide what to eat, when to sleep, where to go—and when to return.

Many child-care experts feel that the authoritative parenting style helps a child to learn best how to think responsibly about her own actions. This sort of discipline is aimed at helping the child control herself—which includes thinking for herself—and is not simply a means of asserting parental control. Being told "Don't play in the street because a car might hurt you" encourages her to think about the consequences of an activity and to take a part in choosing the right course of action; such a statement is therefore far more effective than the frustrating "Don't play in the street because I say so."

Explanation and example

When you take the time to explain the reasons why specific kinds of behavior are bad and good, your child benefits in other

Parent to Parent

When Children Resist

❝ 'I'll do it in a minute,' is Gavin's great line. Whenever we ask him to take the garbage out or straighten out his room, he procrastinates. One day it occurred to me that his line is a pretty clever one because he's not saying he won't do it, just that he wants to do it when it's convenient for him. I decided this was fair, that he has a right to decide his own schedule. But I learned to say, 'Okay, give a specific time when you will do it.' ❞

❝ It never occurs to our seven-year-old, William, to pick up things in his room—even when we think it's in a state of chaos. We range from reminders to threats to get him to clean his room. The one threat that works is 'You do it or we'll do it for you, and we will throw out what we think is unimportant!' We discovered that his idea of cleaning up is to arrange what he thinks is important neatly on his toy shelves; the rest of the items in the room get pushed under the bed or dumped in his brother's room. At least it's better than nothing. ❞

❝ We made a deal with Alex that we would get him a kitten if he would take care of it. But, of course, there have been mornings when he has complained that he doesn't feel like feeding Panther. We remind him that he needs to hold up his end of the bargain and that we will give the cat to someone who will feed it if he won't take the time. We have also asked him to think about how he would feel if we said that we didn't feel like making breakfast for him. ❞

❝ Brian often griped about having to do household chores like the dishes or vacuuming, but he would eventually comply. One day, after spending forty-five minutes vacuuming the house, he asked if he would be paid for his effort. I was surprised by this new request and found out that his friends were getting paid by their parents for various chores. I explained to him that in our house every person in the family needed to make a contribution to the household. I must say that it was very satisfying to have him understand my reasoning and to have the problem resolved. ❞

❝ When Casey turned six, she started throwing a fit if I asked her to change her school clothes before going out to play. She would act in total dismay and try to make me feel that I was making an unreasonable request. I would ask myself, 'Am I asking too much of this child?' No, I decided, it was a reasonable and practical rule, and we worked out a consistent routine. I'd say 'I'll fix your snack while you change, then you can go out and play with your friends.' With the reward of a snack and the thought of having fun outside, she would willingly put on her playclothes. ❞

❝ Colin came home with a report card with top marks for all categories except the one for following class rules. We asked him why, and he answered, 'The rules are dumb.' He said he did not like the rule of having to stop a project when the teacher said he had to. We agreed with him that some rules might seem dumb but pointed out that the teacher needs to have rules to run her class and explained that even grownups had to follow rules—even if they thought the rules were not always good rules. He accepted our explanation and it was never a problem again. ❞

ways. By hearing you state your values clearly, your youngster begins to adopt those values himself. He also becomes better able to weigh the pros and cons of a situation when he finds himself pressured by his peers to do something counter to what he has been taught.

Your task is made easier by the fact that you can now engage your child's cooperative spirit by appealing to the reasoning abilities that develop so dramatically in middle childhood. For example, if he is mature enough to understand reciprocity and fair exchange, you can encourage your youngster to invite a friend over by reminding him that the friend has had him to his own house several times.

Know, too, that it will be easier to teach your child self-discipline if your behavior is consistent with the verbal messages you give him. Since your child will continue to identify strongly with you in middle childhood, he will model much of his moral behavior after what you say and do. If you discourage his making fun of others and then make derisive comments about someone's physical appearance, do not be surprised to hear him react similarly later on.

Firm limits and appropriate disciplinary responses

Your school-age child will probably, at one time or another, test your limits when it comes to permissible behavior. Typical misbehaviors of middle childhood include experiments with lying, cheating, and stealing; and many children resist authority simply by refusing to comply with instructions. The toddler who volunteered eagerly to help you around the house may turn into the recalcitrant child who continues playing catch with his friends instead of taking the few minutes necessary to do his assigned chores; the same child who marched off to bed with a minimum of fuss when younger may now procrastinate endlessly at bedtime and then oversleep the next morning and miss the school bus.

Children need to know what behavior is expected of them and what is forbidden; discipline will be most effective if you have gone to the trouble of spelling out the rules and consequences as well as the reasons for them. It is also important that you monitor your child's behavior regularly and that you are consistent in your responses to his actions. If you tell him to have his toys picked up in ten minutes, then you should follow through by checking back ten minutes later to see that he has complied with your request. Your effort to discipline your child will be ineffective if you wait several days to inspect his room and then suddenly punish him for something he thinks must not be so important, after all. Both you and your partner should agree on your rules and expectations, and you should support each other's decisions so that your youngster cannot play you against your spouse with cries of "But Daddy said I could have some," or "But Mommy lets me do that."

No parent is a saint, and mothers and fathers who intend to use gentle reasoning may lose their tempers at times and fall back on authoritarian methods. Your approach to discipline may occasionally be inconsistent, but do remember that physical punishment may not halt a child's behavior; it may just prompt him to be more careful about getting caught and spanked.

Experts say that when your child misbehaves you help him

most by administering discipline that is appropriate to his misdeed. For instance, restricting after-school playtime for a youngster who nightly returns home past the family's dinner hour will focus the child's attention clearly on his future responsibility for coming home on time.

The effect of discipline on academic progress

Discipline techniques that are based on reason do more than produce superior results in terms of mature behavior. Studies have shown that children disciplined by authoritative mothers and fathers, whose methods are rooted in reason, fairness, and a desire to communicate with their offspring, perform better in school than children who are subjected to harsh authoritarian discipline. Just as cognitive development affects moral development, the right kind of moral training can be a major influence on overall intellectual growth by encouraging youngsters to think independently, to recognize the consequences of their actions, and to see themselves as competent, self-controlled members of the society at large. ∴

Sharing and Caring

Learning good behavior involves more than simply learning not to lie, cheat, steal, and commit other antisocial acts. In middle childhood, your child will become increasingly aware of the importance of positive actions, such as cooperating, sharing, expressing sympathy, and helping others in need. As he matures, with your guidance and example he will move increasingly away from the self-centeredness of his earlier years to a growing concern for the individuals around him. And his growing ability to empathize, to recognize when his behavior is likely to hurt you or his friends, and to put group needs and the needs of other individuals ahead of his own self-interest in certain cases will influence his actions toward others.

Cooperation and competition

Learning cooperation can be an especially difficult task in a society that values and rewards competition to the extent that American society does. Competition and cooperation are both useful forms of social interaction and each has its place in your child's daily life. Everyone must be able to compete and to cooperate with others as the occasion demands, and most children learn both modes of behavior from an early age. Team sports, for example, teach them that victory is achieved by cooperation with teammates as much as by competition against the rival team.

In contemporary North American culture, however, competition is stressed far more than cooperation. When researchers observed children from several different cultural backgrounds playing a board game designed so that cooperation offered the only strategy for success, many of the North American children raised in cities chose the losing competitive approach rather than the winning cooperative one. They had been conditioned to the idea that competing is the best and fastest road to victory. Not even a desire to win was enough to make them try working together as an alternative tactic. Furthermore, the older they were, the less cooperation they demonstrated.

With the social pressure placed on your school-age child to act competitively, you may find it harder to teach cooperation than any other form of altruistic behavior. But by encouraging him to think of himself as cooperative, you can help create a self-fulfilling prophecy. And by engaging him in play such as catch or seesawing, you can demonstrate to him that cooperating can indeed be fun.

Altruism and cognitive development

Like the development of your youngster's moral reasoning, the development of her altruistic behavior and readiness to cooperate with others is linked to the growth of her cognitive skills. While even a toddler may be willing to help a person in need, your school-age child's ability to identify another individual's problems increases during middle childhood as she learns to recognize loneliness, grief, or other difficulties. At the same time, she becomes more adept at offering sympathy or help.

Not only must your child have acquired enough life experience to know what kind of action will help a friend in need, she must also believe that the help is within her power to give. For example, if a classmate's house has burned down, your youngster cannot comfort her friend by rebuilding the house, but she may wish, perhaps as a result of a suggestion by you, to give the friend one of her stuffed animals to replace a similar one lost in the fire. Knowing what kind of help is appropriate and possible is an important part of her learning how to behave in an altruistic manner.

Like the good friend that he is, a boy takes a moment to help out his less-skilled buddy. When encouraged by parents and teachers to cooperate and share, a youngster gradually adds empathy to his repertoire of positive behaviors.

Influences that encourage unselfish behavior

The influences that instill cooperation and altruism are the same ones that shape a child's moral reasoning. As in all areas of character formation, the example of parents and other important grownups in her life makes a deep impression. Adults who behave unselfishly and demonstrate concern for others are extremely influential role models. By volunteering some time for church, school, or neighborhood activities, or by otherwise taking an active role in community affairs, you can demonstrate to your child that you regard giving of yourself as an important feature of your life. You can also teach by suggesting opportunities for altruistic behavior to your youngster. You might point out, for example, just how his behavior can affect other people: "If you invite him to the party, he'll feel good about being part of the group." "You can cheer her up by letting her play with that toy for a while." Teachers can use a similar approach in the classroom, and they can promote cooperative behavior by giving group assignments that encourage the children to work together and to depend on one another for success.

Reward and reinforcement

Rewarding cooperative or altruistic behavior is another successful technique for influencing your youngster. The most effective reinforcer that a child can receive is praise. Genuine words of praise from a loving adult can go a long way toward inspiring a child to repeat altruistic or cooperative patterns of behavior. Remember, however, that you should keep the praise specific: "I'm proud of the way you shared your toys in the sandbox" will be far more effective than "You were very good and generous today."

True altruism grows from the heart. While younger children may respond well to praise, many older children will have come to believe that behaving unselfishly is right and, as such, needs no reward. In other words, they have become convinced that virtue is its own reward.

The important thing for you as a parent, throughout this period of your child's moral development, is to make sure that you treat him as a unique human being. In doing so, you will be modeling the very qualities of empathy and sensitivity to other people's feelings that you wish your youngster to adopt. ❖

For the benefit of their community, these young cub scouts are giving up their Saturday playtime to work alongside their troop leader on a park cleanup project. In middle childhood, children develop a growing sense of social responsibility, especially when influential adults provide examples of altruistic behavior.

Taking On Responsibility

Your goal of making your child a responsible person is partly achievable once she begins demonstrating that she has both the ability and the persistence to take on and finish certain chores. She will probably have already shown that she is capable of handling small amounts of money and of having a say in some family decisions. By allowing her to take on more responsibilities, you will be contributing immeasurably to her self-esteem and giving her new confidence and pride. Soon she may even be able to work outside the home, perhaps delivering newspapers or watering a neighbor's garden.

Working alongside your child

Doing chores can help your child feel like a mature family member who is making a much-appreciated contribution to the household. It is common for a toddler or preschooler to be enthusiastic about helping you, because she likes your companionship and wants your praise. You can encourage increasing responsibility by letting her experience some of the work involved in jobs she will later carry out single-handedly.

Even when your child is ready for greater household duties, she will need your encouragement and supervision. To make it easy for her to get the hang of what she is supposed to do, break each job down into a series of smaller jobs. Loading a dishwasher, for instance, involves cleaning the table off, scraping the dishes and rinsing them, putting them in the racks, adding the soap, and turning on the machine. To teach this process, you can start your child off by asking her to help you clear the table; add more tasks as her capability increases.

Be patient and realistic about your child's work. The first time she makes her bed, she may take a long time and the results may be lumpy and crooked, but praise her for her effort rather than finding fault with the imperfect results. At the same time, though, expect her to do her best and to take pride in her work. Speed and quality will improve with practice, and your attention doubtless will foster a positive attitude toward her responsibilities. As your child becomes more adept at her chores, you can gradually decrease your participation. For example, start out working alongside her as she straightens up her room, and then move on to supervising. Soon you will be able to switch to keeping her company as she works. Eventually, you can leave her to carry on alone, checking her progress only occasionally, or inspecting the job after she is done.

Distributing chores equitably

As a way to reduce your child's grumbling over his assigned chores, be sure to distribute them fairly. Make sure that he gets

to do the fun jobs as often as the unpleasant ones. Not all chores are enjoyable, and while accepting that reality as part of the price of growing up, your child should by no means feel that he is always getting stuck with the job that nobody else wants.

Also see to it that your helper experiences a variety of chores not limited by gender stereotypes. The boy who learns to cook and sew and the girl who learns to handle a wrench and screwdriver are better prepared for adult life than children who learn only a narrow range of traditional male or female skills.

Chores as a means of encouraging responsibility

By entrusting your growing child with more control over his own household work schedule, you can reinforce his developing sense of personal responsibility. Planning and following through with commitments provide as valuable a learning experience as doing the chores themselves. Instead of telling him to put down the book he is reading and clean the bathroom at once, you might give him a list of chores that must be finished by lunchtime, or before the weekend. If he neglects his assignment, discuss the situation calmly and try to arrive at a mutually agreeable solution. Perhaps he needs to set aside a certain time for his chores each day, or perhaps you can help with reminders on laundry or trash day. Be consistent and firm in your discipline for his failure to take care of his various jobs. Using additional chores as a punishment may only reinforce his belief that work is drudgery. Instead, you might withhold a privilege, such as watching television, until the task of loading the dishwasher or taking out the garbage has been completed.

Taking responsibility for money

Taking responsibility means more than helping out at home. It also means developing an understanding of money and being able to handle it wisely. Consider giving your child an allowance starting at the age of five or six, and increasing it as she grows older. How much money you give her depends on several factors, including family finances, local custom, and the expenses it is supposed to cover.

When you have decided on a sum, refrain from criticizing her for the way she uses it. She may wish to spend her allowance from week to week on small treats, or save it up for a few special purchases. Since the purpose of an allowance is to let a child take responsibility for her money, do not tell her she has to save. But if she is saving for an expensive toy or game, avoid destroying her motivation by buying the item for her. The sense of achievement she gains from reaching a personal financial goal will be a powerful influence on subsequent financial issues.

Being part of family decisions

As your child begins to accept more responsibility for household chores and money, he deserves to participate in certain family decisions. Should you take a camping trip this summer or rent an oceanside cottage? What expenses should you cut back on in order to buy a new dishwasher? Your youngster will be affected by these decisions one way or another, so make him part of the discussion as you plan a course of action. Listen to his suggestions, and when you find that you must reject his ideas, explain why. Participation helps your child to learn what is involved in adult decision making and lets him feel that he has a stake in family plans. Some experts believe, too, that if he feels involved, he will be more likely to cooperate with you in implementing plans that affect every member of the family. ❖

Making Difficult Decisions

As your youngster approaches adolescence, he will be confronted with dilemmas that will challenge him to the utmost. Should he try alcohol, especially if his friends are drinking it? Smoke marijuana? Experiment with harder drugs? You may find it difficult to believe that an elementary-school child could face such crucial issues, but substance-abuse statistics leave no doubt that young children are indeed being forced daily into making decisions concerning such matters. According to some studies, the average age at which youngsters first smoke marijuana has fallen to twelve years, and the average age at which they begin drinking alcohol is even earlier—eleven and a half years.

Such temptations can be deadly when faced by children who are not yet able to assess the risks involved and who overvalue the importance of impressing their peers. By arming your child with strong decision-making skills that will permit him to see a problem clearly, come up with a number of possible solutions, and evaluate each of them so that he can pick the best one, you can reduce his chances of making a wrong choice. He can, of course, use these same skills to deal with other problems, large or small. The earlier and more consistently you encourage him to develop a resourceful approach, the more he can fall back on his strength when confronted with a problem, including those times when you will not be nearby to help him. The following pages outline a model for effective decision making that researchers have developed from studies of children who do cope effectively; it is a model that you may wish to use.

As doubtless you recognize from your experiences with your own child, children entering the years of middle childhood possess rudimentary skills for decision making and problem solving. With your gentle prompting and encouragement, even your six-year-old can identify what is bothering him and find ways to deal with it.

Opening lines of communication

Essential to your youngster's developing such coping skills is good, open communication. By encouraging her to feel comfortable talking about problems she faces—from playground teasing to confusion over a teacher's instructions to peer pressure in a patently dangerous situation—you are demonstrating that you take her problems seriously and that you are willing to help her face these often painful issues. But more important than that, your discussions should take place in an atmosphere that not only encourages mutual respect, but also permits everything to be laid out on the table. At such times your listening skills may count for more than your wisdom *(page 65)*.

102

The first thing your child must be able to do in any problem-solving process is to identify the problem. Often this entails sorting through her own feelings, as well as being sensitive to those of others. Teaching your child to be aware of her own emotions may involve showing her how to recognize the physical symptoms that sometimes accompany them. Perhaps her tension manifests itself as queasiness in her stomach or as muscle tightness in her neck and shoulders, or maybe she becomes flushed and dizzy when confronting a situation that frightens or embarrasses her. If she feels a headache or an upset stomach developing as she studies for a big test, use sympathetic questioning to draw her out about the emotions behind the discomfort. Ask what makes this test especially intimidating. Is there some aspect of the subject that she is having particular trouble understanding? Has she felt the same way before?

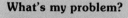

What's my problem?

The kids in the club say I have to steal cookies to be a member. My parents tell me I shouldn't steal. I think stealing is wrong.

I could steal cookies.

I might get caught, or I would get in the club and feel guilty.

I could refuse.

I won't get in the club and may have to find new friends.

I could tell them I don't want to steal, but I could make cookies instead.

They could let me into the club or say no.

I could buy them but say I stole them.

They might catch me, or I'd get in the club but feel guilty.

What is my goal?

I'd like to be a member of the club, but I want to obey my mother and father and do what's right.

What are some of the things that I can do?

Solving a Problem Step by Step
Middle childhood is an ideal time to encourage your child to develop effective problem-solving strategies. Good problem-solvers rely on a systematic approach involving identifying the problem at hand, setting a goal, devising and evaluating a number of solutions, and choosing the one that best meets that goal and presents the fewest potential risks. The youngster shown here uses this method to solve a problem typical of middle childhood; it is a technique that she can continue to use throughout her life.

What will I do?

I'll bake the cookies and hope that they'll let me in the club.

At times you may want to use a more subtle approach to get your child to open up about problems she is facing. Suppose, for example, that you and she have just seen a movie or television program in which one of the characters is a young person with a drug problem. You can take this opportunity to ask her whether many of her schoolmates use drugs, and what she would do if a friend pressured her to try some. If your child feels uncomfortable talking about herself in such a context, you can pose the issue in terms of other children: "Do you know any kids who are under pressure to use drugs? How do you think they could handle the problem?" She may be more comfortable in talking about others than in discussing her own feelings directly.

Identifying a problem may also involve some analytical thinking on your child's part. If she is depressed about not getting a role in the school play, you can help her think through her reaction and put her finger on what is really bothering her. Is she hurt because she feels rejected by a favorite teacher who is directing the play? Does she feel bad because she wants to be recognized for her acting talent? Does she have friends in the play and wish she could share with them the fun of rehearsals?

When helping a younger child identify a problem, you might have to focus your questions a bit: "Are you feeling kind of sad?" "Is this what you're worried about?" With an older child, you can shift to more open-ended questions: "What do you think the problem is?" "How does that make you feel?"

It is vitally important not only for your youngster to understand her own emotions, but also to understand and empathize with another individual's emotions and perspective. To get her thinking this way, when an opportunity presents itself, ask her how she would feel if she were someone else. Perhaps she has temporarily abandoned an old friend in favor of a new friend who has just moved to the neighborhood; but now, as she tries to renew the friendship, she finds the child walks away from her. She interprets this as meanness, but if she has learned to think about nonverbal messages, she may tell you that her friend will not look her in the eye. When she realizes—possibly with some prompting from you—that such a reaction could indicate that the friend is hurt, rather than angry, she may well come to see that she is to blame for having ignored her and then be in a position to make amends.

Setting a goal   Once a youngster is able to identify a problem successfully, the next step in solving it is to have a goal. When your youngster has a clear idea of what she wants to have happen in a given

The Facts of Sexual Abuse

Once a taboo subject, sexual abuse has in recent years come to be recognized as a serious and all-too-prevalent problem. According to some surveys, as many as one out of five women and one out of ten men recall being sexually abused as children. And in some 80 percent of the cases, the abuser is someone the child knows and trusts.

By talking to your youngster frankly but reassuringly about sex and personal safety and by offering her guidelines for action if someone attempts to abuse her, you can reduce the chances of her becoming a victim. Tailor your discussions to your youngster's age and level of understanding. Here are some specific things you can do:

● Make conversations about sex matter-of-fact and as reassuring as you can. Be sure that you both feel comfortable

enough with the subject, so that your child will not be too embarrassed to come to you if something happens.

● To avoid being unduly frightening, you should warn your youngster about sexual abuse in the context of discussions about such basic personal safety measures as taking care when crossing the street or avoiding dangerous machinery.

● Be certain that she understands the difference between a "good touch," one that feels loving and reassuring, and a "bad touch," one that feels uncomfortable or painful.

● Explain to your youngster that you do not expect her to obey every order or request made by an adult. Encourage her to use her judgment and trust her

instincts when a suggestion seems wrong to her—even if the person making it is someone she knows.

● Ask your youngster what she would do if a stranger offered her a ride, for example, or if a grownup she knew asked her to touch his penis. Help her to think of a number of assertive responses such as yelling no and walking quickly away. Without overdoing it, have such what-would-you-do conversations frequently enough that your child feels self-confident.

● Encourage her to come to you immediately and tell you what happened if she has indeed been approached, and reassure her that she will be believed when she does and will not be blamed.

situation, she will be in a better position to make a satisfactory decision. In some cases her goal may be clear. For instance, when she is having difficulty understanding material her teacher has explained to the class, she knows that she wants to grasp it. Other situations may present her with conflicting goals that leave her in a quandary. If her friends have been experimenting with drugs and ask her to join them, she may instantly recognize the need to say no, yet at the same time also feel a need to preserve their friendship. Finding a solution that satisfies both goals may at first elude her. But if she calls on her imagination to help, she may come up with a good one.

Generating alternative solutions

For a child facing such a dilemma, the important thing is to run through a couple of possible solutions before acting. Telling on her friends or saying critically "No way! You must be jerks" would likely satisfy her goal of not taking the drugs but not the other goal of maintaining the relationship. Instead, she might decline in a firm, friendly manner that preserves good feeling and communication: "I'm really not interested. I have to stay straight if I want to get good grades this year." Or "I'd like to be friends, but I don't want to do that. I'm training to try out for basketball this year." Alternatively, she might seek new friends who share more of her own values or avoid socializing with her old friends in situations where drugs might be used.

As part of the decision-making process, a child must be able to examine her own feelings and draw upon her imagination to come up with the kinds of options that will enable her to make the right choice. You might help her along the way by asking her what she feels like doing, how she handled similar problems in the past, or how she thinks some personal hero or role model might behave in a similar situation. She need not generate a huge number of options, but she should consider more than one solution, for she needs to learn that problems can be solved in various ways and that she can have solutions to fall back on in case her first try fails.

Any activity that stimulates creative thinking will further promote a child's ability to generate alternatives, so be alert for opportunities to encourage your youngster to exercise her moral reasoning. Again, if the two of you happen to be watching television together, you might talk about what a particular character has done and ask her what other action the character might have taken instead.

Evaluating possible solutions

Once your child has considered several possible solutions, he has to evaluate their potential effectiveness. For adults, this evaluation is often an automatic part of the process, but for your child, it requires a studied effort to ask himself the kinds of questions that take outcomes into account. "Will I feel okay about my decision later?" "If I do this, will it get me where I want to be a week from now?" "Will this help me get what I really want?" "How will my friends feel if I say or do that? Will they be hurt?" Since it is critical that your youngster learn to weigh positive and negative outcomes, you might want to remind him from time to time of the results certain behavior on his part is likely to produce. You might suggest to him, for instance, that however much he may want to be popular at school, if he goes off with his friends without calling home beforehand, he may end up in hot water with you. Explain that meeting a goal can occasionally bring about unpleasant results and that some goals are therefore worth rethinking.

Choosing a solution and judging the results

The next step, choosing a solution, flows naturally from the process of evaluating the available options. A younger child may need parental help in choosing a solution from the several she has considered, while an older child will be more likely to make the choice herself after weighing the pros and cons.

After she has chosen a solution and acted on it, your child should follow up by assessing the results. Did the solution enable her to achieve her goal? Did it produce the consequences she expected? Were there unanticipated results? Is the problem really solved now, or does she have to take further action? By all means, encourage your youngster to remain flexible and to rethink a solution if it fails. A child needs very much to know that setbacks or failures are often only temporary obstacles on the path to success.

Modeling problem-solving skills yourself

You offer your child his best example of problem-solving strategies put to work. Although many of them are standard, almost unconscious parts of your own decision-making repertoire, take opportunities to think them through aloud for his benefit. When a woman cuts in front of you in line at a crowded grocery store, for example, you might discuss later some solutions to the problem—from the silly (such as punching her) to the serious (such as tapping her on the shoulder to tell her that she has made a mistake and that you were already in line there). Tell him how you evaluated the relative merits of these solutions, and how you came to choose the most sensible response. He will, of course, have already seen the results: After being addressed by you, the woman recognized her error and shifted her cart behind you.

But not all problems can be solved so easily, and sometimes solutions do not work. Let your youngster see that you respond to failures with a positive attitude. As you demonstrate to him again and again that applying problem-solving techniques can be a special and exciting challenge, you offer him a powerful model of persistence to carry into adulthood. ∵

Confronting the Drug Menace

It is a sorrowful but nonetheless real fact of life that some children in late middle childhood and early adolescence begin using alcohol and other drugs. They do so for a variety of reasons. Their natural curiosity, coupled with the ready availability of intoxicating substances, can be one potent motivating factor. They are also strongly influenced by peers and often feel a deep need to establish their grown-up status and independence from parental authority. They may even use drugs as a way of expressing anger and getting back at authority figures with whom they have conflicts. Sometimes they turn to drugs to escape from painful emotions or alleviate stress caused by problems with family, friends, or school. And sometimes the desire for short-term pleasure simply outweighs concern about long-term consequences.

Drug abuse prevention can begin in the early-childhood years. Here are some things you can do:

- Help your child develop character traits and thinking skills that will enable her to resist negative pressures and make wise choices.

- Teach her the importance of taking responsibility for her actions and of facing her own problems squarely.

- Encourage your child to develop her talents and pursue special interests such as music and sports. The more fulfillment and happiness she achieves for herself, the less need your youngster will feel to seek chemical stimulation or euphoria.

- Educate yourself about all aspects of drugs. Keep up-to-date on the popular drugs of the moment, familiarize yourself with drug culture jargon, and learn the medical facts.

- Talk straightforwardly with your youngster about the effects of drugs. Acknowledge that they do give pleasure, and be realistic about the price they exact.

- Find out about drug education efforts at your youngster's school. If there is no special program already in place, then talk with school officials about starting one.

- Educate your youngster by your example. If you drink alcohol or take prescription tranquilizers or painkillers, for instance, let her see that you use these drugs responsibly and not as an escape.

Weathering Childhood Stress

Your child's life will be filled with new and intense pressures in the middle childhood years; from his natural desire for peer acceptance to his striving for academic success, he will be putting forth heroic efforts to master a bewildering array of challenges on the playing field and in the classroom. And as if that were not enough to contend with, your child will most likely bump into a real and unhappy truth during middle childhood: Some of the stable family or neighborhood supports that he relies upon may seem wobbly and less permanent than he imagined. Without a history of weathering such storms and a repertoire of mechanisms for dealing with change and putting things into perspective, your child will be especially vulnerable to stresses brought on by divorce, the family's move to a new neighborhood, or the arrival of a sibling.

Children respond to stress differently. Some bounce back with relative ease even from a severe accident or other family crisis, while others are thrown into a panic by a bad grade on a spelling test. No child is invulnerable to stress, but psychologists have found that some children are exceptionally resourceful and resilient. These youngsters are able to reach into themselves for the strength to survive a difficult situation. You can encourage such positive traits in your youngster so that the pressures and stresses of middle childhood will seem less arbitrary and frightening to him. And by not pushing your youngster to excel in every aspect of his life, you can reduce at least one common major source of pressure.

Letting children be children

Parental expectations can weigh heavily on a child. Remember, your youngster really wants to please you, and he will go to great lengths to gain your approval. He does not need you bearing down on him. A child who constantly feels an obligation to perform for friends and family may feel he is expected to grow up too quickly and may inordinately fear failure. Psychologist David Elkind has referred to youngsters who are pushed academically, socially, or athletically as hurried children.

By all means, encourage your child continually to do his best, and bolster him with honest praise and constructive comments to help him achieve; but do not burden him with blame or disapproval if he is not an *A* student in every class, the top player on every team, the star of every school play, or the most popular guest at every party.

Recognizing stress symptoms

Even children who are not pressured to be prodigies or over-achievers often have to handle a great deal of stress as they strive

to cope with family, friends, and school. Marked departures from normal behavior that continue for more than a few weeks can alert parents to a child under stress. Some children may respond by expressing extreme worry about the present and fear of the future. Others may respond with displays of guilt and anger or with extravagant shows of toughness and bravado. Still others may manifest a sudden lack of interest in things that once sparked their enthusiasm or show signs of a lingering sadness that may signify depression, a condition that requires immediate attention *(box, page 112)*. Sometimes stress produces physical symptoms, especially headaches. Should your child exhibit any of these signs, do not jump to conclusions. Headaches, odd behavior, and other symptoms may have underlying physical causes, so check with your pediatrician first before concluding that the problem is stress related.

If you determine that your youngster is indeed a victim of stress, you can help her to cope positively. Try to be patient with her, to understand her level of mental and emotional development; overlook, rather than punish, misbehavior caused by stress. Keep your expectations for her reasonable, but gently prod her to pursue her schoolwork and household chores as best she can, if for no other reason than to prevent her from buckling under pressure, which could set a precedent for helpless behavior later.

As always, the simple act of listening to a youngster's concerns can ease her mind. Hearing her complaint, you

On moving day, these best friends bid a regretful farewell before movers begin loading household belongings of one of the girls. Since children tend to form closer, more intimate friendships in middle childhood than in the preschool years, moving can produce significant stress for a school-age child as she leaves behind her neighborhood pals.

may see an opportunity to straighten out any misconceptions she may be harboring. When discussing with her a stress-producing family crisis, be honest about your own feelings and about what you think each member can expect from the situation. If you lose your job, for example, explain frankly how the family finances will be affected and what treats and luxuries everyone will have to give up until you find new work. Do not try to hide unpleasant realities, but do not hesitate to clear up misunderstandings and to allay unrealistic fears. Parents can admit to a child that divorce is painful, but they can also explain that they both still love her, and that she will still have ample time with each of them.

Often a child will heap blame on herself for a divorce or an illness in the family. To prevent your youngster from developing such a notion, help her to deal with stress realistically and positively, free of destructive self-blame. In a situation involving a major family disruption, explain clearly that the problems are by no means her fault; she should know, too, that she need not feel it is up to her to devise a solution.

Getting at what is bothering your child

Remember, of course, that your youngster will not necessarily volunteer her every upsetting thought, nor will she always be able to put her finger immediately on what is bothering her. If she is more reticent than some children, you may need to persuade her gently to share with you what is on her mind. She may be ashamed of some of her feelings, such as resentment of a new baby or anger at a parent's remarriage; she might even believe that you will get angry at her for revealing her thoughts. Reassure her that what she is going through is normal and that many children have similar reactions.

When your child is unable to share her distress with you, look for ways to find out its source. Observing her play may give you some clues; you may find her quietly explaining her difficulties to the family dog, for instance. Listen carefully, too, to what she says to others. After a new baby arrived on the family scene, one seven-year-old girl told one of her mother's visiting friends, "The new baby gets everything." Teachers, too, can pick up on a child's distress in the classroom. You may wish, therefore, to set up an appointment with your youngster's teacher and invite him to share his insights with you.

Factors that help a child handle stress

When faced with hardships, people generally focus their attention on the problem itself, looking for solutions, or on their emotions, seeking to understand and accept their own feelings. Resilient people—adults and children alike—rely on both ap-

---

"What I Do When I'm Blue"

"I lie on my bed and stare out the window, thinking about things."
12-year-old girl

"I go up to my room to be all alone except for my cat. I like to pet and play with her."
10-year-old boy

"I watch television—it takes my mind off my problems."
11-year-old girl

"If the weather is good but I feel blue, I go outside to ride my bike as fast as I can."
9-year-old boy

"Something sweet to eat always makes me feel better."
7-year-old girl

"I like to paint because the colors are fun to mix."
10-year-old girl

"I visit my pony in her barn and talk to her about my problems."
12-year-old girl

"I play the piano—the music makes me feel better."
12-year-old girl

"I sit down and read a book."
8-year-old boy

proaches, focusing on the problem and its solutions in situations over which they have some control, and on their personal reactions where they have no control, as in the divorce of parents or the death of a loved one.

Choosing the appropriate response and bouncing back from crises and hardships require a good self-image. For your youngster to have the courage to face up to problems, failures, and the knocks and bruises of daily life, he needs your support, particularly as it enables him to cultivate a healthy attitude toward himself. Experts suggest that children who cope the best have a powerful sense of individuality and a belief that they can exert personal control over their destiny. You can enhance these attributes in your child by bringing him up to believe that he is a special individual, not just an extension of you. Continually reinforce in him the notion that his ideas and goals matter.

You can further prepare your child for dealing with stress by providing a core of stability and order in his life. Even severe problems such as alcoholism in the family or the breakup of a marriage will not overwhelm a child's ability to cope if his daily life provides rituals and routines on which he can depend. Holiday celebrations, prescribed mealtimes and bedtimes, regularly scheduled outings, and assigned chores are all important.

Researchers have found that having a warm, secure, loving relationship with someone is a major dynamic in coping. In many cases that person is a parent, but for many other children that special someone is a grandparent or perhaps a caring adult

In a close moment of sharing, a girl strolls along the beach with her grandmother. Children experiencing stressful events often find that grandparents and other adults outside the family can provide valuable counsel and consolation when the stresses of family and school accumulate.

such as a teacher, coach, or scout leader outside the immediate family circle. Be aware that your child's social contacts increase during middle childhood and that he does not have to rely exclusively on you for support. And in certain circumstances someone else may be better able to offer it than you.

Coping over the long haul

Understand that stress-caused reactions do not disappear overnight. If your youngster is feeling severe inner pressure, he may behave in ways that try your patience and resolve. More than ever, let him know that you love him and that he can count on you. Because family crises are hard on adults as well as children, you may find yourself having to deal with your own stress while ministering to your child. In such situations children often respond with love of their own, providing solace to a beleaguered parent. Still, it is important that you rely primarily on yourself and other adults for emotional support at such times. You may be able to shoulder a share of your child's burden, but do not expect him to carry yours, even a small part of it.

Psychologists know that compassion and concern for others provide an especially strong defense against stress. Through the empathy you display in your own life, you will be providing your child with an example of loving behavior. When he has discovered that caring about the suffering and travail of others is fundamental to being a good human being, he will have gone a long way toward acquiring a powerful means of vanquishing stress whenever it arises in his own life. ∴

Children Who Become Depressed

Just as adults can become seriously depressed, so can children. Because people generally do not think of young children as being subject to depression, they may overlook the symptoms of the condition entirely. Depression is, of course, a difficult problem to assess, but it is nevertheless one that can devastate a child when it strikes. While depression is especially common among teenagers, it also afflicts children in the elementary-school grades.

Left untreated, childhood depression can lead to severe psychological disturbances, even to suicide. It is essential, therefore, that parents be watchful for symptoms of depression in their children, and that they know how to help.

When mental-health professionals talk about depression, they are not referring to the ordinary sadness and disappointment that everyone experiences from time to time, but rather to a dense cloud of misery that can envelop a youngster, fill him with a sense of worthlessness, and at its worst rob the child of his will to make decisions and his desire to live his life.

The causes of depression are both physical and psychological. It can be brought on by, among other things, a traumatic experience, emotional setbacks, or by malnutrition or a chemical imbalance in the brain. Whatever its origin, depression in a child is a serious condition that demands a prompt, effective parental response.

Children who are suffering from depression show many signs that can alert parents to the problem. A depressed child may mope around, constantly blaming and accusing himself, constantly putting himself down. His eating and sleeping habits may undergo major change. He may exhibit misbehavior, stress-related physical ailments, or an intense fear of going to school. He may even become preoccupied with death. Talk of suicide should never be taken lightly; and parents should never hesitate to call hot lines or seek professional help when a child exhibits signs of deep depression.

If your child needs counseling or therapy for depression, you should explain to him what will take place and how the process will aid him. Let him know that you love him and that you want him to feel better. Do not dismiss his problem by telling him to "shape up" or "snap out of it." Once he is receiving treatment, you can help the curative process along by encouraging your youngster to cultivate his abilities and talents so that he can achieve success in school and in other areas of his life.

Coping with Childhood Fears

Middle childhood is a time when many of the fears that troubled your preschooler begin to fade. In a process similar to your child's abandonment of cherished magical explanations for everything from Santa Claus to the moon's particular habit of following her around, her fright of monsters and menacing shadows disappears as her understanding of the world shifts. She may become afraid that you will suddenly fall sick or die or that you and your spouse will divorce. Later on, when peer relationships become more important to her, she may be overly concerned about being disliked or rejected by her classmates. And at the same time, her increased awareness of international events may lead her to fear the threat of nuclear war or the destruction of the environment through pollution.

Such anxieties and fears are part of growing up, of maturing intellectually, and meeting the world on its own—often imperfect—terms. For the most part, they are universal, which means that most youngsters around the globe share a number of fairly typical scary fantasies *(chart, pages 114-115)*; only when such fears persist for a month or so and become so severe that they disrupt the child's daily life do they warrant closer examination.

Responding to your child's fears

Although a six-year-old's vivid belief that the dark is inhabited by ghouls may seem silly to you, it is very real to the child himself. Encourage him to explore in depth what he is feeling, and when possible, try to help him pinpoint the source of his fear. Do not persist, however, if for one reason or another he seems reluctant to talk; and never criticize his fearfulness. If he comes to you to say that a monster is lurking in his closet or under his bed, reassure him that this is not so, and then prove it by opening the closet door or getting down on your hands and knees to peek beneath the mattress. Pooh-poohing a child's fears will do nothing to dispel them; it will simply make the youngster feel foolish—and all the more vulnerable. Next time, he will probably keep his feelings to himself rather than sharing them and thus dispelling his anxiety.

In many cases, exposure to other children who have confronted their fears can be a gentle means to get a child to cope with his. One mother, whose son had a fear of the water, told him that she would pay for a series of swimming lessons if he would go and watch the class. Only a few sessions passed before the youngster, emboldened by the friendly support of the instructor, dared to learn how to swim. In tackling a fear, it helps also to tell a fearful youngster stories about imaginary children who deal successfully with their own apprehensions.

When a child is gripped by senseless fear

Fears can develop into phobias—exaggerated, irrational reactions to anything from snakes and spiders to airplanes. A phobia might lead a child to panic at the sight of a benign garter snake in the backyard, or even of a snake depicted in a book or on television. Some children experience physical reactions, including palpitations and fainting spells. The disturbing thing is that a child who develops a phobia begins to organize his life around it. In the case of a fear of dogs, he might make elaborate plans to avoid any situation in which he might meet up with one, refusing to walk by a certain neighbor's house without holding your hand or to accompany you on a visit to a friend who has a canine pet. In extreme cases, the phobia can take over a child's life to such a degree that it severely limits his freedom of action and deprives him of many of the experiences he needs to grow up successfully. When this happens, treatment is in order; counseling can get at the heart of the phobia and eliminate it.

Conquering phobias

Psychologists suggest that a child can confront and eventually eliminate a phobia by learning some simple relaxation techniques. With an adult standing by, the youngster terrified of snakes might start out by trying to relax as she conjures up in her imagination a serpent, say, dangling from the branches of a tree in a far-off tropical rain forest. She could then progress to looking at caged snakes, or to watching another child play with one. Next, properly encouraged and supported, she could be coaxed into touching or handling a harmless specimen, all the while striving to relax as a way of keeping her panic under control. After a number of exposures, the youngster is likely to overcome her phobia.

Common Fears of the School-Age Child

Cocky though they can seem, school-age children may harbor fears that mirror their growing awareness of their surroundings. A six-year-old will imaginatively pin his fright on things that go bump in the night, but a ten-year-old replaces such scariness with general anxiety over his own success.

One of the most interesting facets of childhood fears is that they may not represent a child's real-life traumas. A fear of snakes, for instance, appears nearly universal, even among youngsters who have never seen one up close.

As your child's skill and knowledge increase, he will be less fearful because he has greater control over events.

Fears at 6 years

- The dark
- Supernatural beings— witches, ghosts, bogeyman
- Separation from parents or loss of mother
- Becoming lost
- Staying in empty house or sleeping in bedroom alone
- Minor injuries—small cuts, bruises, splinters
- Monster or person hiding under bed
- Natural forces—thunder, lightning, water, fire
- Strange noises

When school itself inspires intense fear

A less exotic fear that affects one out of every fifty children at the elementary-school level is school phobia. It is only normal that youngsters have some anxieties that are connected with school, but this phobia extends beyond ordinary anxiety and often manifests itself in vomiting, headaches, and other physical symptoms that appear when the youngster confronts having to go to school.

The reasons for school phobia vary. Sometimes children develop the fear as a result of a teacher's criticism, classmates' taunts, or a bully's threats; often, onset of the phobia may relate to a parent-child struggle for control. For example, a youngster whose mother has just started working outside the home may try to force her back into the role of full-time homemaker and caregiver by developing various physical symptoms and then insisting that he be allowed to stay home.

Sometimes parents can handle the problem by themselves, but other times they may be better off seeking professional help. Easing a child's school phobia, of course, depends on its severity and the source of the fear, and an important task should be to identify the source so that you can work out a solution. Again, permit your child to voice his feelings without criticism, and if necessary, help him come to grips with his fear by arranging for him to speak to the teacher or a school administrator, who can offer reassurance and help in dealing with the problem. Whatever the specifics in a given case, experts caution that it is a mistake for parents to respond to a child's fears by allowing him to remain at home. Sending the youngster to school conveys the message that he should face his problems squarely rather than trying to avoid them. ∴

Fears at 7 to 8 years

- The dark—attic, cellars, dark pits
- Supernatural beings
- Shadows that might be ghosts or witches
- Physical injuries
- Staying alone
- Being tardy for school
- Media reports of wars and disasters
- Burglars, person hiding in closet
- Failure at school

Fears at 9 to 12 years

- Animals, especially snakes and wild animals
- School exams and tests
- Death by nuclear war
- Being singled out for unacceptable physical appearance
- Social rejection
- Physical injuries
- Burglars, murderers, and other criminals
- Natural forces and hazards—thunder, lightning, fire, deep water

Your Youngster's Physical Self

"My, how you've grown!" is a litany your child is likely to hear as she progresses through the middle years of childhood and beyond. And with growth comes a new look, new abilities, new challenges—and a new self-consciousness. Your daughter may fear she is too tall, while your son frets that he will never be tall enough. Children of all descriptions worry that they are the wrong shape. You can do much to allay such fears, reassuring your youngster that she is growing quite well, and ensuring healthy growth with good, nutritious food. And you should make sure your child knows about the most startling of the changes these years bring: the early signs of sexual maturity signaling the start of puberty.

With gains in size also come new strengths and skills, producing satisfaction in many physical activities, be they individual athletic pastimes or organized team sports. Whatever your youngster's skill level, you can find an activity that offers physical fun and exercise. The girl opposite, for example, is enjoying teeball, a version of baseball in which a big tee planted at home plate replaces the pitcher.

Keep in mind that although your child's capacities have grown, they are still limited; to best nurture her athletic development, you must match your expectations to her abilities. When you help her set attainable goals, you help build her self-esteem.

No two youngsters grow at exactly the same rate or into the same shape—particularly during the elementary-school years, when children become increasingly differentiated. But as the following pages tell, there are predictable sequences in the broad outlines of development. As always, the more you know about what to expect, the easier and happier will be the transitions for your child and for you.

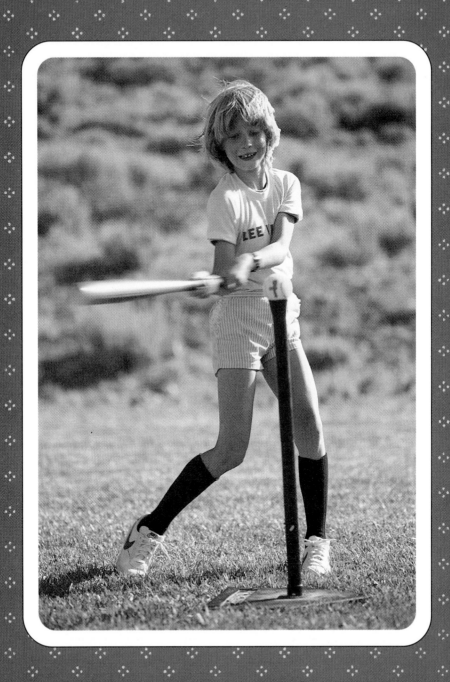

Changing and Growing

During each of their elementary-school years, most children gain an average of five pounds and grow two and a half inches. Thus, by the time they are twelve, they will have roughly doubled their weight and added a third to their height. You might think, from the way you have to keep buying your school-age child new clothes and new sneakers, that he is growing more rapidly now than ever. The truth is he grew faster as an infant and as a preschooler. In fact, studies show that between his sixth and twelfth birthdays, the average child grows only a twelfth as fast as he did in early childhood.

But the growing that your child does during these years will alter his overall appearance even more markedly than it increases his size. As he enters elementary school, his body proportions will have already begun to change; he may have shed most of his cuddly baby fat and outgrown the cute top-heaviness of toddlerhood. During the elementary-school years, his legs and arms continue to lengthen while his torso extends much more slowly, giving him a more adult-looking physique. At the same time, his facial features take on new, more grown-up proportions. The bridge of the nose develops, the cheeks lose much of their roundness, and the jaw widens as baby teeth drop out and are replaced by larger, permanent molars and incisors.

It is easy for you to see that your child's bones are growing longer and his muscles stronger. But other, less visible physical developments are also taking place within his body. His heart becomes more efficient at pumping blood and his lungs increase their capacity. As a result, he becomes physically stronger and can go for longer periods without rest.

Improved motor skills

Along with greater endurance come steady gains in your child's motor skills—his ability to control and coordinate the movements of his arms and legs, hands and feet. At the gross motor level, his control over the large muscles of his arms and legs develops noticeably. As each year passes, he can run faster; jump farther; and throw, catch, and kick a ball with greater power and accuracy. Similarly, as he gains more control of the small muscles in his hands and fingers, he can do better at the fine motor skills; those tasks that require dexterity and precision. His handwriting, once large and awkward, grows smaller and neater, and his drawings are more detailed. He can also play a musical instrument or build model airplanes with increasing facility.

Developing motor skills

Some children are more physically agile than others. This may be innate, or it may have to do with opportunity. One child may

During the elementary-school years, a child's growth is slow compared with his first five years, but it brings dramatic changes. The boy opposite, seen in two views six years apart, was forty-eight inches tall and weighed fifty-two pounds when he was six years old (near right). By the age of twelve (far right), he had not only gained fourteen inches and forty-six pounds, but also a new, near-adult appearance.

have the advantage of being able to learn and practice gross motor skills. The youngster who takes swimming lessons on a regular basis will likely be a better swimmer than the child who occasionally splashes around in the water. Her skills will develop even further if she can practice them on a swim team.

Lessons and practice time are, of course, not the only contributors to a child's mastery of physical skills. Her physiological makeup and such factors as body size and muscle development also play a role, as do her energy level, aggressiveness, and ability to persist at a task. Since school-age children hone many of their motor skills in active play with their peers, it is important that they have plenty of opportunities to participate in group sports. Your child's involvement with a team will nurture her budding social skills as well as improve her athletic ability.

It is now known that there are actually few differences in motor skills between boys and girls during the elementary-school years. Studies do show, however, that boys tend to exhibit greater strength than girls but that the girls outperform the boys in feats requiring balance and coordination. This may partly be a result of cultural influences, with the boys encouraged to participate in challenging team sports and the girls directed into less aggressive activities such as dance and gymnastics. In order to overcome cultural stereotyping, every child should be allowed to develop her own innate physical skills in ways best suited to her particular nature and physique.

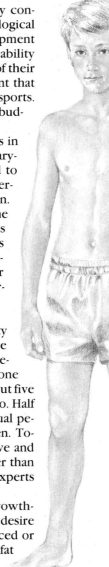

Children today are growing taller and reaching puberty earlier than their parents and grandparents did. In the United States, the average height of schoolchildren between the ages of six and fifteen has been increasing by one inch each decade, making today's average schoolchild about five inches taller than the average schoolchild of fifty years ago. Half a century ago, most girls experienced their first menstrual period between the ages of thirteen-and-a-half and fourteen. Today, menstruation is more likely to begin between twelve and twelve-and-a-half. Boys, too, reach sexual maturity sooner than used to be the case. To explain why this is happening, experts point to improved nutrition and medical care.

Almost any of these changes—whether sex- or growth-related—can make a youngster feel uncomfortable. His desire for conformity may lead him to think himself too advanced or too underdeveloped for his age, too tall or too short, too fat or too thin. Research has shown that many children

When Children Have a Hard Time Paying Attention

As children grow, certain temperamental differences may become apparent that set a few of them apart in the classroom and make them difficult to teach. Some youngsters are, of course, naturally calm and quiet, others much more active. Although such traits are usually apparent from babyhood, they are accentuated in the elementary-school years, when the pupils must concentrate on tasks for long stretches of time. Most children can focus on school tasks with little or no problem. But for a significant number of them—about five percent—such concentration is very hard, if not impossible. These are children with attention deficit disorder, known as ADD.

Of children who are diagnosed as ADD sufferers, between 80 and 90 percent are boys; and most of these boys are hyperactive. They are constantly restless, inattentive, and impulsive. Some ADD children, however, are hypoactive, exhibiting a very low activity level, and apt to daydream excessively; most of these youngsters are girls. Doctors do not know what causes ADD. Some possible, but unproved, explanations include head trauma or a lack of oxygen during birth, low blood sugar, and excessive exposure to lead. Heredity may also play a role, as attentional disorders appear to run in families.

ADD children tend to be of average or above-average intelligence, but because of their behavioral problems, they usually do poorly in school. This is especially true of hyperactive youngsters, whose constant movement and chaotic behavior can also make them unpopular among their peers and can lead to angry and repeated conflicts with parents and teachers. Children who are hypoactive, on the other hand, are usually quiet and compliant and as a result, their difficulties in concentrating are often overlooked by teachers and parents alike.

Children with ADD need clear boundaries at home and at school. Parents can help by setting limits for their child, spelling out what behavior is acceptable and what is not. They can also help by minimizing distractions in the home environment and by teaching the child how to break down tasks into several easy-to-do portions. The ADD child often feels overwhelmed when confronted with a multistep activity, even a fairly simple one such as preparing a report for school.

Psychotherapy can be a helpful treatment for some ADD children, particularly those whose inability to concentrate arises from emotional distress. Another treatment possibility involves using behavior modification techniques. Some medical experts recommend treating both hyperactive and hypoactive children with stimulant drugs. These help both the underactive and the overactive child by allowing them to filter out distracting stimuli and focus on the task at hand. Using drugs to treat attentional disorders is controversial, however. Critics claim the drugs dull the child's mind and can impede, rather than enhance, his ability to learn. The drugs also may have significant side effects, such as diminishing appetite and slowing physical growth. For this reason, many doctors advise that children be taken off these drugs during school vacations.

Parents should be aware that the term *hyperactive* is often misapplied. Half of the parents surveyed in studies in Canada and the United States considered their children to be overactive. It is important to realize that many people regard a child's normal activity level as being too high. A diagnosis of ADD should be considered only after all other environmental and physiological causes for behavioral problems have been excluded. If after carefully monitoring your child's behavior at home, you think you have good reason to believe that he may be an ADD sufferer, talk to his teacher and consult his pediatrician. Once a diagnosis has been made, you can take the necessary steps to help him.

whose bodies depart from certain physical ideals tend to be teased and rejected by their classmates more often than those of average height and build. According to some studies, the most popular boys and girls are generally those with a tall, athletic build, known as a mesomorphic body shape. Less popular are ones with the round and chubby, endomorphic body type, or the thin and underdeveloped, ectomorphic physique. Body shape may also be related to a child's personality. Analysis of available data has suggested that mesomorphs tend to be outgoing and confident; endomorphs, passive and compliant; and ectomorphs, sensitive, introspective, and moody. But the cause-and-effect relationship here is unclear. Some researchers believe

Juggling is easy for some youngsters and harder for others, but fun for everyone. As eye-hand control, dexterity, and other motor skills improve steadily during the elementary-school years, children enjoy growing mastery of many sports and activities.

matching personality traits are inherited along with body type; others think they develop in response to stereotyped expectations. Thus, the mesomorphic child who becomes a leader at school or the endomorphic child who becomes the class clown may just be living up to the expectations of his classmates.

Of course, many children with round or thin physiques are perfectly happy and well-adjusted and are quite popular with their agemates. These children usually have a strong sense of self-esteem and a positive attitude toward their bodies. Parents can help a child value his body by making him feel a delightful person in his own right, even if he is convinced that he differs

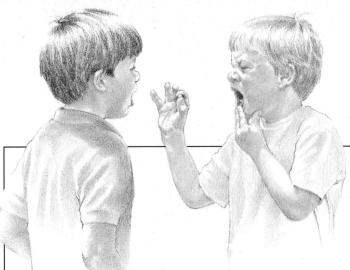

Having just shed his first baby tooth, a young boy proudly shows the result to an admiring friend. Children often look on this initial loss as a visible sign that they are growing up.

Toward Good Dental Care

Between the ages of five and six, your child's jaws expand and the roots of the twenty primary, or baby, teeth dissolve to make way for the thirty-two permanent teeth, shown at right. First to appear are the first, or six-year, molars, which come in behind, but do not displace, any of the baby teeth. Often mistaken for baby teeth, the first molars may be lost if given improper care; this can seriously impair a child's future dental health because these teeth help determine the shape of the lower jaw and the alignment of other permanent teeth. During the next twelve years or so, the remaining permanent teeth appear, culminating in the arrival of the third molars, or wisdom teeth. To protect his new teeth, teach him how to floss and to use a flouride, antiplaque toothpaste. Sometimes a baby tooth fails to fall out when it should and may have to be surgically removed to allow room for the one underneath; sometimes a tooth is lost prematurely, creating a gap that causes other baby teeth to shift and forces the permanent tooth to come up in the wrong spot. To prevent displacement, the dentist can insert a space maintainer in the gap. Some permanent teeth, however, still grow in crooked, are unevenly spaced, or protrude; orthodontic treatment is then required if the problem is to be corrected.

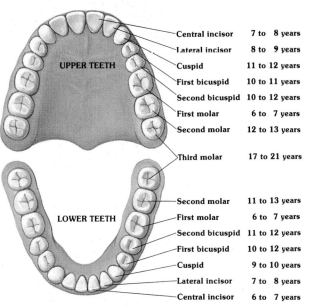

UPPER TEETH	
Central incisor	7 to 8 years
Lateral incisor	8 to 9 years
Cuspid	11 to 12 years
First bicuspid	10 to 11 years
Second bicuspid	10 to 12 years
First molar	6 to 7 years
Second molar	12 to 13 years
Third molar	17 to 21 years

LOWER TEETH	
Second molar	11 to 13 years
First molar	6 to 7 years
Second bicuspid	11 to 12 years
First bicuspid	10 to 12 years
Cuspid	9 to 10 years
Lateral incisor	7 to 8 years
Central incisor	6 to 7 years

from others in his physique, and by encouraging him to be fit, no matter what his shape or size.

Eyes and ears   As the developing child goes on with his schooling, certain physical problems, such as nearsightedness, that existed when he entered school but went unnoticed may now become apparent. His inability to see the blackboard clearly—or to hear the teacher well — will require attention. Sometimes such difficulties come on suddenly, and a child who could read the blackboard quite easily in September may have to take a seat closer to it by December in order to see it. To be on the safe side, have your child's hearing and vision checked every year.

Be alert for signs of problems. Your child may reveal vision difficulties by leaning close to a book or desk while reading or writing, by shutting or covering one eye, or by complaining of blurred vision. You may also see him backing away from objects to see them more readily, squinting, frowning, blinking, or rubbing his eyes frequently. Signs of hearing loss include turning the radio or television up very loud, shifting the phone receiver from ear to ear, and asking to have quietly spoken words repeated. Children who have a family history of deafness or who had frequent ear infections when younger are at increased risk for hearing problems.

Teeth Nothing marks the passage of the elementary-school years more conspicuously than the gaps that suddenly appear in your youngster's smile as he loses his baby teeth. Most children shed the first of their baby teeth around the age of six and the last of them—the canines, or eye teeth—around the age of twelve *(box, opposite)*.

Plan regular visits to the dentist to help ensure good dental health and to detect problems early, when they are easier to correct. Many youngsters develop malocclusions, which may be inherited or brought on by such bad habits as thumb-sucking, pushing the tongue against the teeth, or even breathing through the mouth. The condition keeps the teeth and jaws from coming together properly. One jaw may overlap the other; the teeth may grow in crooked, crowded, spread apart, or otherwise out of line. Some parents mistakenly believe that such problems should not be addressed until the child is a teenager. Intervention at an earlier age, however, is often preferable, for it may avert more serious problems. Treatment for a misaligned jaw, for example, is best done between the ages of six and nine, while the jaw is still growing. And when your child is seven years old, it is not too early to consult your pediatrician and family dentist about the possible need for orthodontia. The process of straightening teeth is costly and inconvenient, but as most of the children and parents who have been through it would agree, it is worth the money and effort. ❖

Many children must wear glasses for better vision or braces for straighter teeth, or, as this boy, both. Understandably, a child may resent being obliged to wear either, but parents can help by explaining the importance of the devices. If your youngster requires such aids, point out how glasses will help him do his schoolwork and how braces will soon give him a more attractive smile. Help him pick out glasses he really likes. And if you can, mention people he admires who have also worn braces.

Sexual Development

The years of middle childhood used to be considered a period of sexual latency. In fact, as you probably are already aware, children of this age group are very curious about sex—particularly their own sexuality. They are not only taken with their physical selves, but also become increasingly interested in members of the opposite sex.

Sexual experimentation

Children express their growing sexual feelings in various ways. Many explore their sexuality in games played with friends or siblings. Six-year-olds may pretend to be doctors and examine each other's bodies, or toss out the venerable challenge, "I'll show you mine if you show me yours!" Such games may involve children of the same or the opposite sex. Seven- and eight-year-olds may peek to see another child or an adult nude.

Parents often worry that the more overt of these activities will lead a child into sexual promiscuity or homosexuality. Such fears, however, are unfounded. Sexual exploration during childhood has not been linked to either behavior in adults, and sexual experimentation is an entirely normal part of childhood. Looking at and touching each other's bodies helps children satisfy a natural curiosity. If you should discover your youngster involved in sex play with another child, try not to overreact. You may wish to steer them into another activity, with a comment such as, "Our bodies are private, so we don't play games like that." When you are alone with your youngster, you might also want to take the opportunity to reinforce your own values, explaining again what the sex act is, and that it is "something grownups do together as a way of loving each other." In any event, avoid punishing your child or making her feel guilty about her sexual experimentation.

Parents should be concerned, however, if their child becomes preoccupied with this kind of play. It may signal an emotional problem. Excessive interest in sexual play can also be a sign that a child has been subjected to sexual abuse. A worried parent should discuss the situation with the child's pediatrician, who may recommend a child psychologist.

Masturbation

Masturbation is another normal and harmless childhood experience for both boys and girls. By the age of three, most children have learned that rubbing or stroking their genitals can cause pleasure. As they grow older, they may masturbate for the relief of tension as well as for the pleasure it brings. A parent's positive acceptance of masturbation as a natural and common experience can go a long way toward making a child feel good about himself and his body. Children need reassurance that masturbatory pleasure is nothing to be worried or guilty about. They also need to know, however, that masturbation, like other sexual activity, should be done in private. If you see your child masturbating in public, quietly take him aside and explain that although there is nothing wrong with touching himself, he should avoid doing it in front of others. Then direct his attention to some other activity.

The onset of puberty As mentioned earlier, the average age at which puberty starts has dropped in recent decades, with most girls menstruating for the first time around the age of twelve-and-a-half and most boys reaching sexual maturity around fourteen. It is not uncommon, however, for these milestones to be passed two years earlier or two years later than the ages set out above. Heredity is the best predictor of when a child will become pubescent; if a mother started menstruating at an earlier-than-average age, for example, her daughter may also.

Although the dramatic physical changes brought about by puberty can appear to set in suddenly, they actually evolve gradually, over a two- to five-year period. Puberty begins when the ovaries and testes receive chemical messages from the brain to increase their production of the sex hormones—estrogen in girls and testosterone in boys. These hormones not only cause the sex organs to mature, but they also stimulate development of a host of secondary sex characteristics, from the widening of the hips in girls to the broadening of the shoulders in boys.

Two twelve-year-olds enjoy dancing together despite a marked difference in heights. Many preteen girls are taller than the boys their age because sexual development, with its accompanying growth spurt, usually begins at an earlier age in the girls.

Early changes in a girl The first sign of puberty in a girl is the slight enlargement of her breasts. This event can happen as early as the age of nine or ten, and is frequently accompanied by a sudden gain in height. After her breasts start developing, the girl will notice the emergence of pubic hair, straight and sparse at first and gradually becoming thicker, coarser, and curlier. Hair does not usually appear under the arms until after pubic hair starts growing, and many girls do not grow underarm hair until after their first menstrual period.

The first period, or menarche, usually follows the first pubic hair by a year or two. Since blood emerging from her vagina is frightening to a girl who has no foreknowledge of menstruation, parents must be sure their daughter knows what to expect beforehand. Menarche shows that a girl's reproductive system is maturing. Remember, however, that normal development is gradual, and establishing a regular monthly cycle may take two or three years. For many girls the initial periods are scant and irregular and occur without ovulation. Other girls, even preteens, may be fertile from the start.

Girls entering puberty have many concerns about the changes in their bodies. They may worry that their breasts are growing unevenly or that they are passing too much blood during menstruation. By talking with your daughter, you should be able to reassure her that what she is experiencing is perfectly normal. Help her regard menstruation positively, as a wholesome function of a healthy body and not a crisis or sickness. Explain that although menstruation may bring some discomfort, she can swim, bicycle, or do any other sport just as actively during her period as at any other time of the month.

Early changes in a boy As with girls, there is often a spurt in a boy's growth just as puberty begins. The first outward signs of puberty in a boy are the enlargement of the testes and scrotum (the sac of skin surrounding the testes). The penis also grows bigger, and pubic hair begins to appear at its base. These changes can occur as early as the age of ten or eleven. About a year after puberty begins, a boy becomes able to produce and ejaculate sperm. He may begin to experience nocturnal emissions, or wet dreams, as his body adjusts to the production of sperm. Parents should tell their son about this phenomenon ahead of time, so that he will not be frightened the first time that he experiences it. Reassure your son that wet dreams are normal, and help him devise a way of dealing privately with wet pajamas and sheets.

Many boys worry at the start of puberty that their penises are not growing large enough or fast enough, or that they are not

The School-Age Child's Changing View of Sex

Your child's notion of where babies come from may surprise you, revealing that although you have given her all the facts, she has altered them to fit her own conceptual framework. But if you are aware of her level of cognitive development, you can supply information to move her closer to the true picture.

A preschooler is apt to say that a baby comes from somewhere else—the baby store or "God's place"—or that he has always been waiting in Mommy's tummy. In their sixth year, most children adopt a "manufacturing" idea, saying that babies are somehow magically assembled. Few connect a father to this process, and many confuse babymaking with digestion.

Point out that babies come from the union of their parents' bodies—sperm from the father's penis joins with an egg inside the mother's body—and that the

baby grows in the uterus, a special place near the stomach but separate from it. Explain that the baby comes out a special opening in the body.

At seven or eight, a child can understand that babies grow from the union of sperm and egg. But she does not see why it must be this way, and she may invent explanations—"the baby comes just by loving." Assure her that while the loving is important, the baby, in fact, comes from the union of two bits of living material. At this age, she may also wonder when a boy can produce sperm, when a girl can have a baby, and why some babies are girls and some are boys.

Many children between the ages of eight and twelve believe that a baby exists preformed, in a sperm or egg, and that it needs the other only to start growing. Explain that there is no baby until egg and sperm have joined, and

that the baby is created from both.

Most youngsters nearing twelve grasp the conception process well, and they may know that unmarried people can have babies. They may ask about more complex matters, such as multiple births, contraception, abortion, and sexual violence. Their concerns also focus on personal choices, values, and relationships, as they wonder what is the right age to have sex. Perhaps some may have anxieties about homosexuality as well.

Throughout your youngster's middle childhood, open and honest dialogue is your best means of making sure she has the facts she needs to make sense of sex and sexuality. If the subject embarrasses you, you may want to say so, but assure your child that sex is a normal, wholesome, private part of life; your positive attitude will help her to keep bringing her questions to you.

---

acquiring enough body hair or muscles. If your son expresses such anxiety, discuss his concerns with him and reassure him that his development is quite natural.

The urgent need for an open dialogue

Toward the end of the elementary-school years, most boys and girls begin to show overt interest in the opposite sex. The days of "Boys are dumb" and "Girls stink" draw to a close, and youngsters may have secret crushes on particular classmates, or even claim someone as boyfriend or girlfriend. With puberty come strong sexual feelings. Parents should realize, however, that not all children of this age are similarly motivated. Some are simply more interested in sports or science than in the opposite sex, while some—possibly about 10 percent—will later develop a permanent homosexual orientation. Parents best foster healthy sexual development when they refrain from pressuring a child into relationships that do not attract him and instead respond nonjudgmentally to his questions and concerns.

If you are the kind of parent who has always talked about sex frankly with your child, you will have laid the groundwork for understanding and continuing discussion during the middle years of childhood and later during adolescence. Such discussion is extremely important, as children are becoming sexually active at a younger age. During recent decades, pregnancies and sexually transmitted diseases among teenagers have risen precipitously. About 23,000 girls under fourteen get pregnant each year in the United States, and millions of young people contract sexually transmitted diseases.

Children's knowledge and values about sexuality should come primarily from their parents. If parents neglect this responsibility, their children are likely to receive incorrect information from peers. Although some schools offer sex education classes, parents can increase the effectiveness of these classes by reinforcing the discussions at home. A trusting, ongoing dialogue with his parents is very beneficial to a child. And it is vital for the parents to understand the child's point of view, if they expect him to accept and incorporate their views and values.

How to approach the subject

Although elementary-school children are deeply interested in sex, they are often reluctant to bring up the topic with their parents. Should you detect such a hesitancy in your youngster, you can get around the problem by using everyday opportunities—a pregnancy in the family, the chance witnessing of animals mating, or scenes on television—to initiate conversations with her about sexual matters. Such casual discussions will let your child know that sex is a normal and important aspect of life and can be talked about comfortably. Be sure to use correct terms for body parts and functions rather than slang or babyish euphemisms, which can confuse a child. And avoid burdening your youngster with more information than she can handle at the moment. Make your answers brief and to the point, and then see whether she has further questions.

What children want to know

Most children need to be reassured that they are developing normally. They want facts about menstruation, masturbation, wet dreams, intercourse, pregnancy, birth control, sexually transmitted diseases, and homosexuality. Sexual abuse is yet another concern. Be sure your child knows the difference between good touching and bad touching, and how to avoid situations that might lead to abuse *(box, page 105).*

Parents must also educate their children about the life-threatening disease of AIDS, or Acquired Immune Deficiency Syndrome. Be frank and honest with your child about the seriousness of the illness, but try not to frighten her. Explain the ways the disease can—and cannot—be acquired. Be sure to place special emphasis on the fact that people do not get AIDS through casual contact with an infected person. If your child has a question about AIDS you cannot answer, just say, "I don't know the answer to that, but I can find out." Then contact a local or national AIDS information resource. ∴•

Building Fitness

Children start out life with the advantage of new bodies, and keeping them fit should be only a matter of fine tuning. But today's reality suggests otherwise. By the time many reach elementary-school age, they are out of shape. Their hearts, lungs, and muscles are not able to function at fullest capacity. As the President's Council on Physical Fitness and Sports has revealed, American children's fitness levels over the past decade have not improved, and in some cases, they have even deteriorated greatly. One out of every four boys and 55 percent of girls cannot do one pull-up. Other studies have shown that nearly one-third of elementary-school children tested were obese. Behind all these statistics is one major cause: simple lack of exercise.

Youngsters nowadays are much less active than children of past decades. Although they may enjoy participating in sports or other physical pursuits, they spend little time at them. This is no surprise, considering that many of them watch an average of five hours of television daily. In addition, large numbers of children must stay at home after school, out of harm's way, until their parents get home from work. Their confinement limits the opportunities for active play.

Children have as much to gain from being fit as adults. Regular exercise builds flexibility and muscle strength, relieves tension, and strengthens the cardiovascular system. It can also enhance a child's self-esteem. The youngster who can run long distances, for example, or do a series of pull-ups has reason to feel good about both his body and himself.

A nutritious lunch, whether prepared at school or brought from home, helps these classmates recharge their energies during the busy school day. Involving your child in the planning and preparation of his lunch will help him learn the basics of good nutrition and meal planning.

Children who are physically fit also are less likely to develop degenerative conditions, such as arteriosclerosis and heart disease, later in life. Early signs of these health problems have been seen in some first-graders. In fact, studies have indicated that 40 percent of children five to eight years of age show at least one heart disease risk factor, including obesity, elevated cholesterol, and high blood pressure. Regular exercise is one of the best ways to reduce these risks.

Although parents often mistake sports skills for fitness, the ability to hit a baseball or throw a football has little to do with true physical fitness, which involves several elements: muscle strength, muscle endurance, cardiovascular endurance, and flexibility. The truly fit child also is in the weight range appropriate for his age and height.

To keep in shape, children need activities that contribute to all areas of physical fitness. Especially important are aerobic activities—those that keep the heart beating at 75 percent of its maximum rate for at least twenty minutes. Swimming, running, bicycling, skating, dancing, jumping rope, and cross-country skiing are all good aerobic exercises for children. Team sports requiring plenty of running, such as soccer and field hockey, can also build cardiovascular endurance. Sports such as baseball, however, in which players stand still most of the time, contribute little to fitness.

To encourage your child to adopt fitness as a lifelong pursuit, make aerobic exercise a regular part of your family life. This can be as simple as taking long walks or bicycle rides together in the evening, or swimming at a local pool. Choose a wintertime aerobic activity, too, such as ice-skating or cross-country skiing. Studies show that more than half of school-age children engage in no physical activities at all during the winter months.

How Fit Is Your Child?

You can gauge your child's fitness by having him do the exercises given in the chart below. Focused on boys and girls ages six to twelve, it comes from the President's Council on Physical Fitness and Sports, a national award program that recognizes outstanding achievement in certain physical exercises by boys and girls ages six to seventeen. The chart includes the five exercises to be performed and scores to be attained or surpassed in order for the children to qualify for the award, a certificate signed by the president of the United States. The scores listed represent the 85th percentiles; that is, of students sampled in a national survey, 15 percent in each age group did as well or better than the scores that are listed below.

Each exercise is designed to test and improve physical fitness. The pull-up—grasping an overhead horizontal bar, raising the

BOYS	AGE	PULL-UPS	1-MILE RUN (min./sec.)	CURL-UPS (timed one min.)	V-SIT REACH OR SIT-AND-REACH (inches +/−)	SHUTTLE RUN (seconds)
	6	2	10:15	33	+3.5	12.1
	7	4	9:22	36	+3.5	11.5
	8	5	8:48	40	+3.0	11.1
	9	5	8:31	41	+3.0	10.9
	10	6	7:57	45	+4.0	10.3
	11	6	7:32	47	+4.0	10.0
	12	7	7:11	50	+4.0	9.8

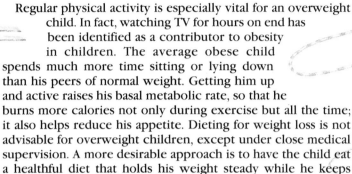

Regular physical activity is especially vital for an overweight child. In fact, watching TV for hours on end has been identified as a contributor to obesity in children. The average obese child spends much more time sitting or lying down than his peers of normal weight. Getting him up and active raises his basal metabolic rate, so that he burns more calories not only during exercise but all the time; it also helps reduce his appetite. Dieting for weight loss is not advisable for overweight children, except under close medical supervision. A more desirable approach is to have the child eat a healthful diet that holds his weight steady while he keeps growing taller. That way he gets all of the nutrients he needs, and his body gradually slims down.

Whether your child is overweight or not, he will benefit from developing sound eating habits early in life. School-age youngsters need three daily servings of low-fat milk or milk products, two servings of lean meat or meat substitutes, four or more servings of fruits and vegetables, and four or more servings of whole-grain breads and cereals. Like adults, children should limit their intake of salt, sugar, and saturated fats. Good nutrition starts with a proper breakfast. Studies have shown that youngsters do better in school and can better resist infection and fatigue when they eat a substantial morning meal. Make sure your child's other meals are balanced as well. When packing his school lunch, be sure to include fresh fruit and a raw vegetable, such as a carrot stick or a piece of celery. Avoid providing cake, cookies, or packaged junk foods as snacks or desserts. Instead, offer your child fresh or dried fruits, cheese and crackers, yogurt, and lightly salted, unbuttered popcorn. ⁂

body until it is chin level with the bar, and then lowering it again—strengthens arms and shoulders. The one-mile run, in which walking is also permitted, invigorates the heart and lungs. The curl-up—touching elbows to thighs with knees flexed, feet on the floor, hands placed on opposite shoulders, and arms hugging the chest—firms abdominal muscles. The sit-and-reach—stretching the arms and upper body forward toward a measuring line, with legs extended, feet apart and toes pointed upward—flexes the hamstrings and lower back. And the shuttle run, focusing on speed and agility, builds a youngster's overall endurance and coordination. In this exercise, two parallel lines are drawn thirty feet apart, with two blackboard erasers placed behind one line and the contestant behind the other. On signal, the contestant runs across the floor, picks up one eraser, returns it to the starting line, then repeats this procedure to retrieve the second eraser and complete the event.

GIRLS	AGE	PULL-UPS	1-MILE RUN (min./sec.)	CURL-UPS (timed one min.)	V-SIT REACH OR SIT-AND-REACH (inches +/−)	SHUTTLE RUN (seconds)
	6	2	11:20	32	+5.5	12.4
	7	2	10:36	34	+5.0	12.1
	8	2	10:02	38	+4.5	11.8
	9	2	9:30	39	+5.5	11.1
	10	3	9:19	40	+6.0	10.8
	11	3	9:02	42	+6.5	10.5
	12	2	8:23	45	+7.0	10.4

Lessons from Team Sports

Team sports are exhilarating, a wonderful way for a child to burn off excess energy and exercise his body at the same time. Many elementary-school-age children enjoy being part of a team, swept up by the feeling of belonging and camaraderie that it brings. They also enjoy honing their skills or learning new ones, whether pitching a fastball or dribbling a soccer ball. But most of all, children just like playing on a team because it is fun.

The value of sports

In the course of the fun, sports can also offer a child many subtle benefits. Her self-esteem grows with her developing athletic skills. As a team member, she learns to cooperate with others, discovering that by helping a teammate score, she helps the team. She becomes comfortable with competing and risktaking, and she learns to take in stride both the excitement of success and the frustration of failure. And she comes to appreciate the value of self-control, practice, and perseverance.

How much a team sport contributes to a child's physical fitness depends a great deal on the coach. Good coaches counsel children on the importance of staying in shape and use practice sessions to build overall fitness as well as specific sports skills. Team workouts can establish lifelong fitness habits. And the good coach instills or reinforces the values of fairness, courtesy, mutual respect, and teamwork.

Readiness for team sports

At what age should your child begin to participate in organized sports? The answer depends on his emotional as well as his physical maturity. Although some six-year-olds can play a sport such as soccer with enthusiasm and ease, others may find it physically too demanding and emotionally too intense. Team play also demands an understanding of rules and concepts that are hard for many young children to grasp, such as the idea of staying in position during a soccer match rather than chasing the ball all around the field.

Although opinions vary, many experts suggest the following age guidelines for competing in sports: A child should

be six to eight years old before starting noncontact sports, such as baseball, swimming, tennis, and track, and eight to ten years old before participating in contact sports, such as soccer, basketball, and wrestling. One who wants to play a collision sport, such as ice hockey or tackle football, should be at least ten to twelve years old before joining a team. Bear in mind, however, that because children can differ greatly in their physical maturity and abilities, the recommendations made here may not necessarily be appropriate for your youngster.

Whatever you do, avoid rushing your child into organized sports, especially the highly competitive ones. Instead, let his interests develop gradually, through plenty of free play with friends, or introduce him to a sport through a beginners' course that stresses skill development rather than competition.

Selecting a sport

If possible, you and your child should decide together which sport he will play. His interests, of course, should be of primary concern in making a choice, although you will also want to consider such factors as safety and the amount of time the sport will demand of him—and of you. Evaluate the various programs available; some will be much more competitive than others. Then sit down with your youngster and talk over the possibilities. Find out what he expects. Does he want to excel as an athlete or simply to spend enjoyable time with friends?

More often than not, children are drawn to the sport in which they have the best skills. If your child shows no preference, try to guide him toward an activity suited to his build, so he will have a better chance of performing well. A shorter-than-average child, for example, may have a tough time competing in basketball but could do very well on the gymnastics team.

Digging in their heels and hauling on the rope, children on a tug-of-war team give the game their best effort. Competitive sports, whether tennis, soccer, or a simple tug of war, offer children fitness and fellowship, especially when parents and coaches emphasize having fun rather than winning.

The Risk, Prevention, and Treatment of Sports Injuries

Because elementary-school children are small, have limited strength, and lack the competitive drive of their elders, they are far less likely than teenagers to suffer serious sports injuries. Bruises, bumps, scratches, and strains are the typical mishaps that befall athletic youngsters of this age, and these are usually caused by their trying to do too much too soon or too fast. Nevertheless, children are sometimes badly hurt, and the risk of that happening depends often on the sport itself.

Playing baseball is especially hazardous because of the danger of being hit by a ball. The most frequent soccer injuries, on the other hand, are blisters, skin abrasions, bruises, or sprains. Among noncontact sports, gymnastics has a high accident rate, although the severity of the injuries is usually relatively minor. The trampoline, however, has been banned by many schools because its use has caused severe head and neck traumas. Probably the safest sport is swimming, where muscle pulls and a mild ear infection known as swimmer's ear are common. In all these sports, overtraining should be avoided; a tired child is more susceptible to injury.

To help prevent injuries on the playing field, competitions should be set up only between youngsters who are evenly matched in size, age, strength, and ability. Children should also be in good physical shape before taking up any sport and should always do warmup and stretching exercises before a game or practice session. The right safety equipment is another must. Helmets, mitts, face guards, padding, and other protective devices should fit properly, be adequately constructed, and be kept in good condition.

When an accident does occur, such as a collision on the field that results in a hurt ankle, the player should be immediately removed from the game with as little disturbance to the injury as possible. First aid should be given before taking the child to a doctor or to a hospital emergency room for examination: Immobilize the wounded area and apply the so-called ICE treatment (ice, compression, and elevation). Wrapping the injured limb snugly with an elastic bandage and placing an ice pack over it will help ease the pain and reduce the swelling. The ice causes any damaged blood vessels to constrict so there is less bleeding. The bandage should not be fitted so tightly, however, that it cuts off circulation. Elevating the injured area above the level of the heart is also important because it drains away excess fluid and promotes healing. If your child is unable to see a physician promptly, the ice and bandage should be kept in place for a half hour, removed for a fifteen-minute interval, then reapplied; this procedure should be repeated for about three hours.

Sports and girls

In past generations, girls had little opportunity to play organized sports. That situation has changed, and most communities today recognize the importance of fitness for girls and include them in their athletic programs. The myth that sports are somehow unfeminine has all but vanished, and girls are no longer scoffed at for wanting to swing a softball bat or play soccer.

Because they are about equal in size and strength, preadolescent boys and girls can play on the same teams and compete against each other. After puberty, when the boys gain an advantage in strength and muscle mass, boys and girls are usually directed onto separate teams.

The role of parents and coaches

Most children make great team players. When problems develop in the games they play, it is often not the youngsters who are at fault, but the grownups. Some coaches become so intent on winning that they lose sight of the main reasons children play sports: to have fun, develop skills, and

make or deepen friendships. Parents, too, may lose perspective, urging children to excel and criticizing them when they fail. Not only does such misguided emphasis ruin the fun and give the players a distorted view of sports; it can lead to injuries. Studies show that youngsters in a win-at-all-costs atmosphere suffer more injuries than those who are allowed to enjoy a relaxed, for-fun style of play.

Your role should be a supportive one. Encourage your child's efforts, whether she makes a line drive hit or goes down swinging. Never demand victory, and do not show disappointment over her performance. Also, consider other avenues to exercise and athletic pleasure; many children do not enjoy team play, preferring an individual sport, such as skiing or tennis.

Make a point of talking with your child's coach. Discuss his approach to sports, and then observe him at games and practices. Does he create a positive atmosphere, giving all of the players plenty of encouragement? During games, does he try to have all of the children participate? Is he respectful of officials and opposing teams? You will certainly not want your child on a team whose coach mistreats children, verbally or physically, or who disparages or berates officials or opponents.

Helping your child enjoy sports

There are many ways, of course, that you can motivate your child and enrich his experiences on the playing field. Show that you care about his activities by attending games and an occasional practice. Take a seat in the spectator area but remember to let the coach do the coaching. And refrain as well from advising your child or his teammates. You should be seen, but not heard, no matter how enthusiastic you may get.

Evenings or weekends, you can help your child learn the fundamentals of his sport. Organize sandlot ball games or mini track meets with other neighborhood families. Make these games fun for everyone; you might top off the event with pizza at a nearby fast-food restaurant. Going to professional games adds another dimension to his sports experience. As he watches the pros, he will see teamwork and also pick up pointers on techniques and strategies. Some teams offer free or inexpensive sports clinics where children can improve their skills and meet a couple of sports heroes. Call the public-relations office of a team near you for information. ❖

Landmarks of Development

	Physical	Information Processing	Cognition	Communication
Six Years Old	Prints letters and numbers smaller, more neatly; can cut out angular pattern such as paper doll. Runs about 32 yards in just under 8 seconds. Can do 3-foot standing broad jump. Learns to roller-skate and to skip (6-8). Throws with proper weight shift, step. Throws ball 15 feet; can catch 8-inch ball bounced from 15 feet.	Begins to have intuitive sense of how memory works: knows recent events are easier to recall, longer lists harder to memorize. Can learn to use rehearsal (repetition) as memory aid. Is able to copy a square and a diamond (6-8). Draws a person with features heretofore omitted—neck, clothing, and hands. Can apply old rule to new problem; can apply opposite of old rule to new problem.	Begins logical, cause-effect reasoning. Still tied to specific experience but does some mental manipulations as well as physical ones. Knows numbers up to 30; differentiates morning and afternoon. Grasps conservation of number: that number of items in each of two equal rows stays same, even after one row is shortened by respacing.	Can think about what she is being told and judge whether message is clear. Speech is fluent, well-modulated, usually phonetically correct. Understands more complex sentences; has absorbed rules of building sentences. Avoids contradicting self. Laughs at ideas that seem incongruous, such as a dog saying meow (3-6).
Seven Years Old	Can discriminate left and right in own body. Can balance on one foot, blindfolded; can walk on 2-inch-wide balance beam. Can jump vertically about 7 inches, can hop accurately; is able to enjoy hopscotch. Gains arm-leg coordination used in jumping jacks. Can start combining physical and verbal skills in such games as jump rope.	Is aware of memory limitations, knows when he has forgotten something; can repeat 5-number series, or 3-number series backwards. Can find camouflaged figures, such as a rectangle hidden within a larger grid. Begins to notice missing parts of familiar figure: might see hand is missing from picture of a man.	Knows basic number concepts and understands that numerals represent number quantities in one-to-one correspondence. Can add pairs of numbers by end of first grade, and can count by 2s and by 5s. Can tell time. Understands conservation of mass: that ball of clay rolled into snake is still same amount of clay (6½-7½).	Can read simple words by end of first grade. Can judge whether what she is being told contains enough information: whether rules given, say, are all those needed to play a game. Understands jokes, puns, and riddles with multiple word meanings.
Eight Years Old	Has enough fine motor control to use most household tools, such as can opener and screwdriver. Can do alternate rhythmical hopping, shifting from left to right foot in 2-2, 2-3, or 3-3 pattern. Rides bicycle with skill.	Can describe from memory similarities and differences between two objects. Uses efficient scanning strategies, as when comparing or searching for objects; can pick out the relevant, ignore the irrelevant. Is less distractable, can pay attention selectively; can do homework even when television is on.	Knows that time refers to a single, constant flow of incidents, marked off by calendars and clocks; can tell day of month and year, is interested in the past. Higher-level intellectual skills are established: can classify items by attribute (such as color), and seriate items by size. Learns that height and width are reciprocal and complementary; that a tall, narrow glass can hold as much as a short, wide one.	Can give adequate simple directions within the home or neighborhood.

136

The chart that begins on these pages traces the major benchmarks of a child's physical, cognitive, and social development between the ages of six and twelve. Developmental rates, of course, vary between children— and between the sexes—and while those presented here derive from studies of large numbers of children, no child matches the resulting timetable exactly. Various behaviors tend to overlap, many begin or end gradually, many can appear years earlier or later than the average. Age ranges for normal onset are in parentheses. Thus, when you consult the chart for your nine-year-old's likely progress, look also at the rows for the eight- and the ten-year-old.

Moral Reasoning	Sense of Self	Role-Taking	Social Relationships (Family, Friends, Peers)
Applies morality of constraint, deciding what is right and wrong on basis of rules: What is punished is wrong. Acts so as to avoid punishment. Regards rules as absolute and unalterable, punishment for violations as inevitable. Believes rules should be obeyed under all circumstances, and that everyone should get same treatment under rules (5-7).	Becomes increasingly aware of self as unique individual. Describes self in terms of physical features, concrete activities. Begins to judge his own worthiness. Begins to feel strong consciousness of self as male or female; knows gender is permanent.	By end of this year, begins to be aware that others may view things differently. Wonders what others think (6-8). Begins to consider own and others' motives. Becomes sensitive to plight of those less fortunate—the poor, the handicapped.	Says friendship consists of sharing toys or fun. Peer groups are hierarchical, dominance-based (6-7). Has rudimentary skills in initiating play; seeks common interests with peers. Confrontations are immediate, direct, often tactless (6-8½). Sees parents as caretaker-helpers (5-9). Respects authority figure's power (5-8).
Moves on to morality of cooperation: through play with peers, comes to see rules as social contracts, subject to negotiation, and obeys rules to get rewards (7-8). In applying rules, can make allowance for special cases, considers merit and reciprocity.	Believes own identity remains constant. Comes to terms with socially prescribed sex-role standards and pressures for conformity (7-12).	Suddenly realizes that another person can think about what he is thinking: "I know that you know that I know" (7-12).	Sees friendship as mutual cooperation; explores similarities and differences between self and friends. Sees parent as counselor, satisfier of needs (7-12). Believes authority figure is owed obedience because of superior abilities or past favors (7-9).
Makes decisions about right and wrong on basis of pleasant outcome, fair exchange. Wants to be thought of as good child. Can weigh person's motives for breaking a rule; finds some breaking of rules justifiable (8-10).	Begins to understand difference between self and body. Evaluates self by comparing self with peers. Feels shame and guilt based on self-evaluation. Begins to discern own and others' personality traits; begins to think of ability as a stable trait.	Understands need to attend to others' frame of reference when initiating play.	Has best friend or chum, shows real sensitivity to chum as a person. Engages in spontaneous but short-lived, same-sex groupings, with leaders and followers, visible jockeying for power. Boys' groups large, girls' smaller, intensive. Respects leadership; believes authority cares about his welfare (8-10). May be demanding, challenging toward parents.

	Physical	Information Processing	Cognition	Communication
Nine Years Old	As fine motor control increases, can enjoy sewing and knitting. From standing position can spring 8 to 10 inches off the ground.	As memory aid, uses classification, organizing list of items according to their attributes.	Understands reversibility, fact that some comparisons imply others: If Ann is taller than Betty, then Betty is shorter than Ann. Grasps conservation of weight: that two equal pieces of clay still have same weight, even if shapes change.	Describes objects in detail, going beyond simply telling what they are used for.
Ten Years Old	Runs 32 yards in 5½ seconds; does standing broad jump of more than 4½ feet. Throws a softball more than 30 feet. Can usually catch small ball thrown from a distance. In girls, first signs of puberty (10-14).	Uses rehearsal, repeating list of items to self, when asked to memorize series; can correctly repeat 6 digits forward, 4 digits in reverse, 20-syllable sentence.	Can use numbers beyond 100 with understanding; can use simple fractions.	Has increasing understanding of nonliteral uses of language; can begin to appreciate metaphors, such as "the ship plowed the ocean."
Eleven Years Old	Can do standing broad jump of about 5 feet.		Considers the future. Understands conservation of volume: that two equal pieces of clay displace the same amount of water, even when their shapes change.	Can define such abstract terms as "justice," "revenge," and "honesty."
Twelve Years Old	Can run twice as fast as at 6 years, having gained about 1 foot per second in speed each of previous 6 years. May be able to execute running high jump of 3 feet. Boys experience beginnings of puberty (12-16).	As memory aid, begins to use elaboration, imagining list items in story or familiar setting. Can memorize random list of 6 or 7 items.	Uses logical, physical explanations of concrete events; begins using deductive (if-then) reasoning. Can manipulate ideas, can imagine and think about things never seen or still in future. Can make map of familiar place.	Knows rules of spelling. Can read and understand complex stories. Can appreciate irony in jokes.

138

Moral Reasoning	Sense of Self	Role-Taking	Social Relationships (Family, Friends, Peers)
Wants to conform to community standards, fit in, be considered good.	Can differentiate multiple selves, such as social, intellectual, athletic, behavioral, physical looks.	Identifies others' emotions based on cues from surroundings: "He's having a birthday, he must be happy."	Says friendship consists of sharing thoughts and feelings (9-10). May express scorn for opposite sex. Is concerned about popularity; desires conformity to peers (8-14). Sees peer group as a culture separate from family.
Applies morality of instrumental exchange: believes that moral action consists of making fair deals and trades.	Includes personality traits when describing self. Understands that personal uniqueness comes from thoughts and feelings as well as actions.	Becomes able to consider simultaneously both own and another's point of view (10-15). Can identify another's thoughts more easily than emotions (10-15). Can take third-person perspective, observe self and another in mutual relationship (10-15).	Prefers group of same-sex agemates (10-15). Regards parents with respect, tolerance; can discuss disagreements (10-15). Complies with leader in spirit of willing consent, cooperation. Gains achievement motivation, strives toward goals.
Uses conventional moral reasoning, focusing on conforming to social order and family obligations. Thinks moral behavior consists of following social rules and conventions.		Identifies another's emotions based on facial cues.	In friendship, says it is important to share problems and give emotional support, trust, and loyalty.
Believes in following rules to maintain mutual respect in social relations, with school, family, peers. A few children may become able to seek conflict resolution in terms of greatest good for greatest number.	Defines self in terms of values, beliefs, private thoughts, and motives.	Begins to see people in societal context, knows that upbringing and personality traits shape behavior (12-15). Seeks explanations for others' conflicting motives and contradictory traits.	Sees friendship as constantly changing and adapting to new situations; realizes that resolving conflict can strengthen a relationship (12-up). Can be friends with more diverse people: opposite sex, different ages.

Bibliography

BOOKS

Ackerman, Paul R., and Murray M. Kappelman, M.D., *Signals: What Your Child Is Really Telling You.* New York: Dial, 1978.

Adams, Sam, Leslie Ellis, and B. F. Beeson, *Teaching Mathematics.* New York: Harper & Row, 1977.

Baron, Bruce, Christine Baron, and Bonnie MacDonald, *What Did You Learn in School Today?* Mount Vernon, N.Y.: Consumers Union, 1983.

Beck, Joan Wagner, *Effective Parenting.* New York: Simon and Schuster, 1976.

Becoming a Nation of Readers. Washington, D.C.: Department of Education, National Institute of Education, Commission on Reading, 1985.

Bernstein, Anne C., *The Flight of the Stork.* New York: Delacorte, 1978.

Brenner, Barbara, *Love and Discipline.* New York: Ballantine Books, 1983.

Clabby, John F., and Maurice J. Elias, *Teach Your Children Decision Making.* Garden City, N.Y.: Doubleday, 1986.

Clarke-Stewart, Alison, and Susan Friedman, *Child Development: Infancy through Adolescence.* New York: John Wiley & Sons, 1987.

Elkind, David, *The Hurried Child.* Reading, Mass.: Addison-Wesley, 1981.

The FCLD Learning Disabilities Resource Guide, by the Foundation for Children with Learning Disabilities. New York: New York University Press, 1985.

Flavell, John H., *Cognitive Development.* Englewood Cliffs, N.J.: Prentice-Hall, 1985.

Fogel, Alan, and Gail Melson, *Child Development: Individual, Family, and Society.* St. Paul: West Publishing, 1987.

Frith, Terry, *Secrets Parents Should Know about Public Schools.* New York: Simon and Schuster, 1986.

Galton, Lawrence, *Your Child in Sports.* New York: Franklin Watts, 1980.

Green, Morris, M.D., and Robert J. Haggerty, M.D., *Ambulatory Pediatrics.* Vol. 3. Philadelphia: W. B. Saunders, 1984.

Harris, A. Christine, *Child Development.* St. Paul: West Publishing, 1986.

Harris, Judith Rich, and Robert M. Liebert, *The Child: Development from Birth through Adolescence.* Englewood Cliffs, N.J.: Prentice-Hall, 1987.

Hetherington, E. Mavis, and Ross D. Parke, *Child Psychology: A Contemporary Viewpoint.* New York: McGraw-Hill, 1986.

Hill, Kennedy T., "Motivation, Evaluation, and Educational Testing Policy." In *Achievement Motivation,* ed. by Leslie J. Fyans. New York: Plenum Press, 1978.

Hooks, William, et al., eds., *Pleasure of Their Company.* Radnor, Pa.: Chilton, 1981.

Ilg, Frances L., M.D., Louise Bates Ames, and Sidney M. Baker, M.D., *Child Behavior.* New York:

Harper & Row, 1981.

Jerman, Max E., and Edward C. Beardslee, *Elementary Mathematics Methods.* New York: McGraw-Hill, 1978.

Kuczen, Barbara, *Childhood Stress.* New York: Dell, 1987.

Leach, Penelope, *Your Growing Child.* New York: Alfred A. Knopf, 1986.

Levine, Melvin D., M.D., et al., *Developmental-Behavioral Pediatrics.* Philadelphia: W. B. Saunders, 1983.

Liebert, Robert M., and Joyce Sprafkin, *The Early Window: Effects of Television on Children and Youth.* New York: Pergamon, 1988.

Long, Lynette, and Thomas Long, *The Handbook for Latchkey Children and Their Parents.* New York: Arbor House, 1983.

McCracken, Janet Brown, ed., *Reducing Stress in Young Children's Lives.* Washington, D.C.: National Association for the Education of Young Children, 1986.

Morris, Richard J., and Thomas R. Kratochwill, *Treating Children's Fears and Phobias.* New York: Pergamon, 1983.

Mussen, Paul H., et al., *Child Development and Personality.* New York: Harper & Row, 1984.

Mussen, Paul H., ed., *Handbook of Child Psychology:*
Vol. 3, *Cognitive Development.* New York: John Wiley & Sons, 1983.
Vol. 4, *Socialization, Personality, and Social Development.* New York: John Wiley & Sons, 1983.

Oppenheim, Joanne, Betty Boegehold, and Barbara Brenner, *Raising a Confident Child.* New York: Pantheon Books, 1984.

Osman, Betty B., *Learning Disabilities.* Mount Vernon, N.Y.: Consumers Union, 1979.

Parke, Ross D., *Fathers.* Cambridge, Mass.: Harvard University Press, 1981.

Rivers, Caryl, Rosalind Barnett, and Grace Baruch, *Beyond Sugar and Spice: How Women Grow, Learn, and Thrive.* New York: G. P. Putnam's Sons, 1979.

Rubin, Zick, *Children's Friendships.* Cambridge, Mass.: Harvard University Press, 1980.

Salk, Lee, *The Complete Dr. Salk.* New York: World Almanac Publications, 1983.

Scarr, Sandra, Richard A. Weinberg, and Ann Levine, *Understanding Development.* San Diego: Harcourt Brace Jovanovich, 1986.

Schaefer, Charles E., *How to Talk to Children about Really Important Things.* New York: Harper & Row, 1984.

Schickedanz, Judith A., David I. Schickedanz, and Peggy D. Forsyth, *Toward Understanding Children.* Boston: Little, Brown, 1982.

Schulman, Michael, and Eva Mekler, *Bringing Up a Moral Child.* Reading, Mass.: Addison-Wesley, 1985.

Segal, Julius, and Zelda Segal, *Growing Up Smart*

& Happy. New York: McGraw-Hill, 1985.

Smith, Nathan J., Ronald E. Smith, and Frank L. Smoll, *Kidsports: A Survival Guide for Parents.* Reading, Mass.: Addison-Wesley, 1983.

Spivack, George, Jerome J. Platt, and Myrna B. Shure, *The Problem-Solving Approach to Adjustment.* San Francisco: Jossey-Bass, 1976.

Swan, Helen L., and Victoria Houston, *Alone after School.* Englewood Cliffs, N.J.: Prentice-Hall, 1985.

Wattleton, Faye, and Elisabeth Keiffer, *How to Talk with Your Child about Sexuality.* Garden City, N.Y.: Doubleday, 1986.

Zigler, Edward F., and Matia Finn-Stevenson, *Children: Development and Social Issues.* Lexington, Mass.: D. C. Heath, 1987.

PERIODICALS

Barko, Naomi, "Conquering Math Malaise." *Working Mother,* January 1988.

Berliner, David, and Ursula Casanova Piñero:
"Are You Teaching Students the Right Skills for Retention?" *Instructor,* February 1987.
"How Memory Works: Implications for Teachers." *Instructor,* January 1985.

Bernstein, Anne C., "How Children Learn about Sex & Birth." *Psychology Today,* January 1976.

Comer, James P.:
"Fathers and Daughters." *Parents,* December 1984.
"The Importance of Body Image." *Parents,* September 1984.
"The Other Sex." *Parents,* September 1987.

Copple, Carol, "Personality Parade." *Sesame Street Parents' Guide,* April 1988.

Dodge, Kenneth A., et al., "Social Competence in Children." *Monographs of the Society for Research in Child Development,* 1986.

Edmondson, Daisy:
"Bullies." *Parents,* April 1988.
"The Surprising Truth about Children's Height." *Parents,* September 1987.

Gardner, Howard, "How Many Ways Is a Child Intelligent?" *Instructor,* January 1985.

Gottman, John Mordechai, "How Children Become Friends." *Monographs of the Society for Research in Child Development,* 1983.

Honig, Alice Sterling, "Humor Development in Children." *Young Children,* May 1988.

Humphreys, Anne P., and Peter K. Smith, "Rough and Tumble, Friendship, and Dominance in Schoolchildren: Evidence for Continuity and Change with Age." *Child Development,* 1987, Vol. 58, pp. 201-212.

Kutner, Lawrence, "Parent & Child: In Dealing with Bullies, Solutions Start at Home." *The New York Times,* May 5, 1988.

McGhee, Paul E., "Children's Appreciation of Humor: A Test of the Cognitive Congruency Principle." *Child Development,* 1976, Vol. 47, pp. 420-426.

Marks, Jane, "There's Got to Be a Better Way." *Parents,* September 1987.

Meer, Jeff, "Remembrance of Things Lost." *Psychology Today,* November 1986.

Moely, Barbara E., and Wendell E. Jeffrey, "The Effect of Organization Training on Children's Free Recall of Category Items." *Child Development,* 1974, Vol. 45, pp. 135-143.

Morton, Caryl, "The Best Way to Talk to Kids." *Parents,* October 1985.

Oden, Sherri, and Steven R. Asher, "Coaching Children in Social Skills for Friendship Making." *Child Development,* 1977, Vol. 48, pp. 495-506.

Pellegrini, A. D., and Jane C. Perlmutter, "Rough-and-Tumble Play on the Elementary School Playground." *Young Children,* January 1988.

Roberts, Marjory, "School Yard Menace." *Psychology Today,* February 1988.

Rubin, Nancy, "Math Stinks!" *Parents,* June 1988.

Russell, Graeme, and Alan Russell, "Mother-Child and Father-Child Relationships in Middle Childhood." *Child Development,* 1987, Vol. 58, pp. 1573-1585.

Rutter, Michael, "School Effects on Pupil Progress: Research Findings and Policy Implications." *Child Development,* 1983, Vol. 54, pp. 1-29.

"Safety for Latchkey Children." *Parents,* December 1987.

Schwartzberg, Neala S., "What TV Does to Kids." *Parents,* June 1987.

Segal, Julius, "Kids Who Bounce Back." *Parents,* April 1988.

Segal, Julius, and Zelda Segal, "Avoiding Sex-Role Stereotypes." *Parents,* December 1987.

Shantz, Carolyn Uhlinger, "Conflicts between Children." *Child Development,* 1987, Vol. 58, pp. 283-305.

Stigler, James W., Shin-ying Lee, and Harold W. Stevenson, "Mathematics Classrooms in Japan, Taiwan, and the United States." *Child Development,* 1987, Vol. 58, pp. 1272-1285.

Trawick-Smith, Jeffrey, "Play Leadership and Following Behavior of Young Children." *Young Children,* July 1988.

Yando, Regina M., and Jerome Kagan, "The Effect of Teacher Tempo on the Child." *Child Development,* 1968, Vol. 39, pp. 27-34.

OTHER PUBLICATIONS

"Child Sexual Abuse: What It Is and How to Prevent It." Elk Grove Village, Ill.: American Academy of Pediatrics, 1988.

"Drug Abuse: Family Enemy Number One." National Federation of Parents for Drug-Free Youth, no date.

Moglia, Ronald, "AIDS: How to Talk to Your Children about AIDS." New York: New York University, 1986.

"National Children and Youth Fitness Study II." Washington, D.C.: Department of Health and Human Services, Office of Disease Prevention and Health Promotion, no date.

"The National Conference on Youth Fitness." Campbell Soup Company, June 1984.

"Orthodontics: More Than Beautiful Smiles." St. Louis: American Association of Orthodontists, 1986.

"The Presidential Physical Fitness Award Program." Washington, D.C.: President's Council on Physical Fitness and Sports, 1987.

Rutherford, George W., et al., "Overview of Sports-Related Injuries to Persons 5-14 Years of Age." Washington, D.C.: Consumer Product Safety Commission, December 1981.

"Self-Protection Lessons for Your Child." Knoxville, Tenn.: Parenting Adviser Information Center, 1987.

"TV and Reading." Washington, D.C.: Reading Is Fundamental, 1985.

Weinstein, Claire, et al., "How to Help Your Children Achieve in School." Washington, D.C.: Department of Education, March 1983.

"When We Were Young." Washington, D.C.: Reading Is Fundamental, 1987.

"Youth Physical Fitness in 1985." Washington, D.C.: President's Council on Physical Fitness & Sports, 1985.

Acknowledgments and Picture Credits

The editors wish to thank: Dr. Carolyn T. Cobb, North Carolina Department of Public Instruction, Raleigh, N.C.; Melva Holloman, Washington, D.C.; Jalna Jones, MacArthur Elementary School, Alexandria, Va.; Laurie McLaughlin, Lafayette Elementary School, Washington, D.C.; Barbara Tomlinson, MacArthur Elementary School, Alexandria, Va.; James Wendorf, Reading Is Fundamental, Inc., Washington, D.C.

Sources for the photographs in this book are listed below, followed by sources for the illustrations. Credits from left to right are separated by semicolons, from top to bottom by dashes.

Photographs. Cover: Roger Foley. 4: Elizabeth Richter—Roger Foley—Elizabeth Richter. 5: Robert Eckert/EKM-Nepenthe—Elliott Smith. 7: Elizabeth Richter. 10: © Julie Habel/West Light. 23: Roger Foley. 61: Elizabeth Richter. 69: © Arthur Tilley 1988. 71: Jerry Howard/Positive Images. 77: Roger Foley. 85: Robert Eckert/EKM-Nepenthe. 93: Roger Foley. 95: © Arthur Tilley 1988. 100: Elliott Smith. 117: Elliott Smith.

Illustrations. 8: Jack Pardue from photo by Kathy Zinsmeister Price. 10: Graphics by Cynthia T. Richardson. 14: Jack Pardue from photo by David M. Kinney. 16: Jack Pardue from photo by Marilyn Segall. 20: Jack Pardue from photo by Kathy Zinsmeister Price. 24, 25: Lisa F. Semerad from photo by Cynthia T. Richardson. 27: Tina Taylor. 28: Lisa F. Semerad from photo by Marion F. Briggs. 30: Lisa F. Semerad from photo by Arthur Tilley. 33: Lisa F. Semerad from photo by Ellyn Sudow. 38: Lisa F. Semerad from photos by Beecie Kupersmith. 39: Lisa F. Semerad from photo by Kathy Zinsmeister Price. 40: Lisa F. Semerad from photo by Marion F. Briggs. 42: Lisa F. Semerad from photo by Beecie Kupersmith. 43: Lisa F. Semerad from photo by Marion F. Briggs. 44: Lisa F. Semerad from photo by Kathy Zinsmeister Price. 49: Lisa F. Semerad from photos by Marion F. Briggs. 51: Lisa F. Semerad from photo © Mark E. Gibson. 52, 53: Marguerite E. Bell from photos by Marion F. Briggs. 54, 55: Marguerite E. Bell from photos by Marion F. Briggs and Kathy Zinsmeister Price. 56-59: Marguerite E. Bell from photos by Marion F. Briggs. 62, 63: Elizabeth Wolf from photos by Marion F. Briggs. 66: Elizabeth Wolf from photos by Marion F. Briggs. 73: Child's art by Danny Newton—child's art by Ivy Al-Faqih. 75: Elizabeth Wolf from photo by Marion F. Briggs. 79: Elizabeth Wolf from photos by Cynthia T. Richardson. 80, 81: Elizabeth Wolf from photos by Marion F. Briggs and Beecie Kupersmith. 82, 83: Elizabeth Wolf from photos by Ellyn Sudow. 86, 87: Donald Gates from photos by Beecie Kupersmith. 90, 91: Donald Gates from photos by Marilyn Segall. 97: Donald Gates from photo by Marion F. Briggs. 98: Donald Gates from photo by Ron Cooper/EKM-Nepenthe. 103-109: Donald Gates from photos by Marion F. Briggs. 111: Donald Gates from photo © Jerry Howard/Positive Images. 114, 115: Linda Greigg. 119: Marguerite E. Bell from photos by Kathy Zinsmeister Price. 121: Marguerite E. Bell from photo © Jerry Howard/Positive Images. 122: Marguerite E. Bell from photo by Marion F. Briggs—Dan Beisel. 123: Marguerite E. Bell from photo by Cynthia T. Richardson. 125: Marguerite E. Bell from photo by Beecie Kupersmith. 129: Marguerite E. Bell from photo by Kathy Zinsmeister Price. 130: Marguerite E. Bell from photos by Marion F. Briggs—Elliott Smith; Cynthia T. Richardson—Marion F. Briggs (2). 131: Marguerite E. Bell from photos by Mark E. Gibson—Mark E. Gibson; Cynthia T. Richardson—Marion F. Briggs (2). 132-135: Marguerite E. Bell from photos by Cynthia T. Richardson. 136-139: Elizabeth Wolf from photos by Marion F. Briggs.

Index